电气工程及其自动化专业英语
(第二版)

Special English for Electrical Engineering and Automation (The 2nd Edition)

主　编　李文娟

华中科技大学出版社
中国·武汉

内 容 提 要

本书分为十六个单元,主要内容包括电路、计算机、模拟电子技术、数字电子技术、电机学、信号与系统、自动控制、电气测量技术、电器设备、电力电子技术、电力系统等。书中内容按每个单元用2学时授课的计划安排,每个单元后都配有主要词汇注释、要点注释和练习等内容,书后还给出了全部练习的参考答案。

本书既可作为电气工程及其自动化、工业电气自动化、自动控制、机电一体化、科技英语等相关专业的专业英语教材,也可作为从事电气工程、电子信息、自动化等相关专业工程技术人员的参考用书。

图书在版编目(CIP)数据

电气工程及其自动化专业英语/李文娟主编. —2版. —武汉:华中科技大学出版社,2019.9(2023.8重印)
ISBN 978-7-5680-5683-0

Ⅰ.①电… Ⅱ.①李… Ⅲ.①电气工程-英语-高等学校-教材 ②自动化技术-英语-高等学校-教材
Ⅳ.①H31

中国版本图书馆 CIP 数据核字(2019)第 204189 号

电气工程及其自动化专业英语(第二版)　　　　　　　　　　　　　　李文娟　主编
Dianqi Gongcheng Ji Qi Zidonghua Zhuanye Yingyu(Di 2 Ban)

策划编辑:刘　平
责任编辑:刘　平
责任校对:封力煊
责任监印:周治超
出版发行:华中科技大学出版社(中国·武汉)　　电话:(027)81321913
　　　　　武汉市东湖新技术开发区华工科技园　　邮编:430223
录　　排:华中科技大学惠友文印中心
印　　刷:武汉开心印印刷有限公司
开　　本:787mm×1092mm　1/16
印　　张:10.75
字　　数:262千字
版　　次:2023年8月第2版第5次印刷
定　　价:36.00元

本书若有印装质量问题,请向出版社营销中心调换
全国免费服务热线:400-6679-118　竭诚为您服务
版权所有　侵权必究

前　言

近些年，各高校普遍对教学进行了改革，重新调整了各专业的课程设置和学时分配。专业英语课程由原来的3个学期压缩至1个学期，学时也由以往的80~90学时调整到现在的28~34学时。在有限的学时中让学生阅读到本专业的主要外文文献资料，掌握基本的专业词汇，提高学生阅读和翻译英语科技文献的能力，是编者编写本书的目的。

本书中所选内容涉及面广，包括电路、计算机、模拟电子技术、数字电子技术、电机学、信号与系统、自动控制、电气测量技术、电器设备、电力电子技术、电力系统等方面的知识。每一部分内容的选取都突出了相关技术最基础的知识，便于电气类相关专业的学生更好地学习和掌握，也有助于学生英语水平进一步提高；同时对非电气类专业的学生也达到普及电气工程基础知识的目的，兼顾了英语和专业学习。

编者结合多年的教学授课经验，在本书选材和编排上，使每个单元的内容均可以在2学时的教学中讲授完。这样一次课一个主题，既清晰明了，又重点突出。本书共有十六个单元，可满足28~34学时授课的需要。

为了便于学习，每个单元后都给出了生词和词汇，同时还针对文中的难点给出了注释。每个单元还精心编写了练习，帮助学生巩固和理解所学知识。练习分为3类：词汇或短语汉译英、根据课文回答问题、句子英译汉，并在书后给出了练习参考答案。

在表示有关"量"的符号时，按原文献给出，一些元器件的符号则按照国际标准给出，特此说明。

本书的编写得到了哈尔滨理工大学许多老师和研究生的帮助，编者在此表示衷心的感谢！

由于编者专业知识和外语水平有限，书中错误和不足之处在所难免，敬请使用本书的广大师生和读者批评指正，本人将不胜感激。

编　者
2007年5月

再 版 说 明

本书自 2007 年出版以来,经国内多所大学使用,广受好评。为了更好地发挥本书的作用,全面提高本书的质量,我们对全书进行了修订。除订正原书的疏漏之外,还充实了本书的内容。关于本书的具体修订工作,特作以下几点说明。

1. 基本保持原书的体系、结构不变。虽然增加了两个单元,篇幅有所增加,但是,本书简明扼要的编写风格依然没有改变。

2. 替换了第 4 单元的内容。第 4 单元用"Computers"代替了原书的"Electronic System"。

3. 增加了两单元的内容并作为第 9 单元和第 10 单元。"Signals"为第 9 单元,"Continuous-Time and Discrete-Time Systems"为第 10 单元。

4. 顺延了原第 9 单元至第 14 单元的内容。原书中第 9 单元至第 14 单元依次顺延为新版书的第 11 单元至 16 单元,这样使读者的阅读范围更广、授课教师的授课内容选取空间更大。

5. 本教材为教师提供教学课件。课件以动画的形式展示了主要生词的音标,更加方便教师授课和学生学习。

感谢国家留学基金资助,感谢 University of Notre Dame 林海博士的邀请,使编者有机会在 University of Notre Dame 访学并聆听到林海博士讲授的课程。编者由此获得了更新内容的灵感和资料,完成了本书的再版工作。

感谢哈尔滨理工大学周美兰教授为本书的出版所做的工作!感谢哈尔滨理工大学硕士研究生韩福强、冷雪为本书绘制的插图。感谢哈尔滨理工大学研究生付天雷、马亮亮、李鼎胜和聂久富为课件制作付出的努力!

感谢华中科技大学出版社刘平编辑对本书再版工作的督促和帮助!

虽然认真地对原书进行了校对,但错误和不当之处在所难免,敬请读者批评指正。同时,借此机会,向使用本书的广大师生致以由衷的感谢!

编　者

2018 年 11 月

于 University of Notre Dame

Contents

Part 1 Basic Concepts of Electric Circuit ··· 1
    1.1 Introduction ··· 1
    1.2 Charge and Current ··· 2
    1.3 Voltage ·· 3
    1.4 Power and Energy ·· 3
    1.5 Summary ·· 5

Part 2 Basic Laws of Electric Circuit ·· 7
    2.1 Introduction ··· 7
    2.2 Ohm's Law ··· 7
    2.3 Kirchhoff's Laws ·· 9
    2.4 Series Resistors and Voltage Division ································· 10
    2.5 Parallel Resistors and Current Division ······························· 11
    2.6 Summary ·· 12

Part 3 Capacitors and Inductors ·· 15
    3.1 Introduction ·· 15
    3.2 Capacitors ·· 15
    3.3 Inductors ·· 18
    3.4 Summary ·· 20

Part 4 Computers ·· 23
    4.1 Introduction ·· 23
    4.2 Computer Function ··· 23
    4.3 Computer Structure ·· 24
    4.4 Classes of Computing Applications ··································· 27

Part 5 Operational Amplifiers ··· 31
    5.1 Introduction ·· 31
    5.2 Operational Amplifiers ·· 31

5.3　Ideal Op Amp …… 34
5.4　Inverting Amplifier …… 34
5.5　Noninverting Amplifier …… 35
5.6　Summary …… 36

Part 6　Digital Logic Circuits …… 39
6.1　Basic Concepts …… 39
6.2　Electrical Specifications for Logic Gates …… 43

Part 7　Transformers …… 46
7.1　Introduction …… 46
7.2　Transformer Construction …… 47
7.3　The Ideal Transformer …… 49

Part 8　Electrical Machines …… 54
8.1　A Brief Overview …… 54
8.2　Induction Machines …… 55
8.3　Synchronous Machines …… 57
8.4　Direct-Current Machines …… 58

科技英语学习要点(一)——科技英语的特点 …… 64

Part 9　Signals …… 70
9.1　Introduction …… 70
9.2　Continuous-Time and Discrete-Time Signals …… 70
9.3　Periodic Signals …… 72
9.4　Even and Odd Signals …… 73
9.5　The Unit Impulse and Unit Step Functions …… 74
9.6　Summary …… 76

Part 10　Continuous-Time and Discrete-Time Systems …… 79
10.1　Introduction …… 79
10.2　Interconnections of Systems …… 79
10.3　Basic System Properties …… 81
10.4　Summary …… 84

Part 11　Automatic Control Systems …… 87
11.1　Introduction …… 87

11.2	Block Diagrams and Transfer Functions		87
11.3	Open-Loop Control		89
11.4	Closed-Loop Control: Feedback		90
11.5	Objectives of a Control System		92

Part 12 Measurement 95

12.1	Introduction	95
12.2	Statistics	95
12.3	Operating Characteristics	96
12.4	Static Characteristics	97
12.5	Velocity Measurement	99

Part 13 Switching Components 103

13.1	Introduction	103
13.2	Mechanical Switching Components	103
13.3	Solid-State Components	106

Part 14 Power Semiconductor Switches 112

14.1	Introduction	112
14.2	Thyristors	112
14.3	Metal-Oxide-Semiconductor Field Effect Transistors	114
14.4	Gate Turn-Off Thyristors	115
14.5	Insulated Gate Bipolar Transistors	117
14.6	Desired Characteristics in Controllable Switches	117

Part 15 Rectifiers and Inverters 121

15.1	Introduction	121
15.2	Basic Rectifier Concepts	122
15.3	Practical Thyristor Converters	124
15.4	Inverter Mode of Operation	126

Part 16 Basic Knowledge of Power System 131

16.1	Introduction	131
16.2	Electric Energy	131
16.3	Fossil-Fuel Plant	131
16.4	Nuclear Power Plant	132

- 16.5 Hydroelectric Power Plant ... 133
- 16.6 Other Energy Sources ... 133
- 16.7 Transmission and Distribution Systems ... 133
- 16.8 Faults ... 135
- 16.9 System Protection Components ... 135

科技英语学习要点(二)——科技英语翻译常用技巧 ... 140
练习参考答案 ... 149
References ... 164

Part 1

Basic Concepts of Electric Circuit

1.1 Introduction

Electric circuit theory and *electromagnetic* theory are the two *fundamental* theories upon which all branches of electrical engineering are built. Many branches of electrical engineering, such as power, electric machines, control, electronics, communications and instrumentation, are based on electric circuit theory. Therefore, the basic electric circuit theory course is the most important course for an electrical engineering student, and always an excellent starting point for a beginning student in electrical engineering education. Circuit theory is also valuable to students specializing in other branches of the physical sciences because circuits are a good model for the study of energy systems in general, and because of the applied mathematics, physics, and *topology* involved[1].

In electrical engineering, we are often interested in communicating or transferring energy from one point to another. To do this requires an interconnection of electrical devices. Such interconnection is referred to as an *electric circuit*, and each component of the circuit is known as an *element*.

An electric circuit is an interconnection of electrical elements.

A simple electric circuit is shown in Fig. 1.1. It consists of three basic elements: a battery, a lamp, and connecting wires. Such a simple circuit can exist by itself; it has several applications, such as a torch light, a search light, and so forth.

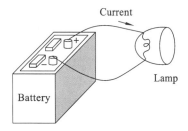

Fig. 1.1 A simple electric circuit

Electric circuits are used in numerous electrical systems to accomplish different tasks. The objective is not the study of various uses and applications of circuits. Rather our major concern is the analysis of the circuits. By the analysis of a circuit, we mean a study of the behavior of the circuit: How does it respond to a given input? How do the interconnected elements and devices in the circuit interact?

We commence our study by defining some basic concepts. These concepts include charge, current, voltage, circuit elements, power, and energy.

1.2　Charge and Current

The concept of electric charge is the underlying principle for explaining all electrical phenomena. Also, the most basic quantity in an electric circuit is the *electric charge*. We all experience the effect of electric charge when we try to remove our wool sweater and have it stick to our body or walk across a carpet and receive a shock.

Charge is an electrical property of the atomic particles of which matter consists, measured in coulombs (C)[2].

We now consider the flow of electric charges. A unique feature of electric charge or *electricity* is the fact that it is mobile; that is, it can be transferred from one place to another, where it can be converted to another form of energy.

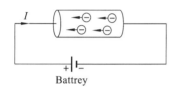

Fig. 1.2　Electric current due to flow of electric charge in a conductor

When a conducting wire is connected to a battery, the charges are compelled to move; positive charges move in one direction while negative charges move in the opposite direction. This motion of charges creates electric current. It is conventional to take the current flow as the movement of positive charges, that is, opposite to the flow of negative charges, as Fig. 1.2 illustrates.

Electric current is the time rate of change of charge. Mathematically, the relationship between current i, charge q, and time t is

$$i = \frac{dq}{dt} \tag{1.1}$$

where current is measured in amperes (A), and

$$1 \text{ ampere} = 1 \text{ coulomb/second}$$

The charge transferred between time t_0 and t is obtained by integrating both sides of Eq. (1.1). We obtain

$$q = \int_{t_0}^{t} i dt \tag{1.2}$$

The way we define current as i in Eq. (1.1) suggests that current needs not be a constant-valued function.

If the current does not change with time, but remains constant, we call it a *direct current* (DC), that is, a direct current is a current that remains constant with time. By convention the symbol I is used to represent such a constant current.

A time-varying current is represented by the symbol i. A common form of time-varying current is the sinusoidal current or *alternating current* (AC), that is, an alternating current is a current that varies sinusoidally with time. Such current is used in the household, to run the air conditioner, refrigerator, washing machine, and other electric appliances.

Once we define current as the movement of charge, we expect current to have an associated direction of flow. As mentioned earlier, the direction of current flow is conventionally taken as the direction of positive charge movement.

1.3 Voltage

To move the electron in a conductor in a particular direction requires some work or energy transfer. This work is performed by an external electromotive force (emf), typically represented by the battery in Fig. 1.1. This emf is also known as *voltage* or *potential difference*. The voltage u_{ab} between two points a and b in an electric circuit is the energy (or work) needed to move a unit charge from a to b; mathematically,

$$u_{ab} = \frac{\mathrm{d}w}{\mathrm{d}q} \tag{1.3}$$

where w is energy in joules (J) and q is charge in coulombs (C). The voltage u_{ab} or simply u is measured in volts (V). From Eq. (1.3), it is evident that

$$1 \text{ volt} = 1 \text{ joule/coulomb} = 1 \text{ newton meter/coulomb}$$

Thus, voltage (or potential difference) is the energy required to move a unit charge through an element, measured in volts.

Figure 1.3 shows the voltage across an element (represented by a rectangular block) connected to points a and b. The plus (+) and the minus (−) signs are used to define the reference direction or voltage polarity. The u_{ab} can be interpreted in two ways: (1) point a is at a potential of u_{ab} volts higher than point b, or (2) the potential at a with respect to point b is u_{ab}. It follows logically that in general

Fig. 1.3 Polarity of voltage u_{ab}

$$u_{ab} = - u_{ba} \tag{1.4}$$

Current and voltage are the two basic variables in electric circuits. The common term *signal* is used for an electric quantity such as a current or a voltage when it is used for conveying information[3]. Like an electric current, a constant voltage is called a DC voltage and is represented by U, whereas a sinusoidally time-varying voltage is called an AC voltage and is represented by u. A DC voltage is commonly produced by a battery; an AC voltage is produced by an electric generator.

1.4 Power and Energy

Although current and voltage are the two basic variables in an electric circuit, they are not sufficient by themselves. For practical purposes, we need to know how much *power* an electric device can handle. We all know from experience that a 100-watt bulb gives more light than a 60-watt bulb. We also know that when we pay our bills to the electric utility companies, we are paying for the electric *energy* consumed over a certain period of time. Thus power and energy calculations are important in circuit analysis.

To relate power and energy to voltage and current, we recall from physics that:

Power is the time rate of expending or absorbing energy, measured in watts (W).

We write this relationship as

$$p = \frac{\mathrm{d}w}{\mathrm{d}t} \quad (1.5)$$

where p is power in watts, w is energy in joules, and t is time in seconds (s). From Eqs. (1.1), (1.3), and (1.5), it follows that

$$p = \frac{\mathrm{d}w}{\mathrm{d}t} = \frac{\mathrm{d}w}{\mathrm{d}q} \cdot \frac{\mathrm{d}q}{\mathrm{d}t} = ui \quad (1.6)$$

or

$$p = ui \quad (1.7)$$

The power p in Eq. (1.7) is a time-varying quantity and is called the *instantaneous power*. Thus, the power absorbed or supplied by an element is the product of the voltage across the element and the current through it. If the power has a $+$ sign, it is being delivered to or absorbed by the element. If, on the other hand, the power has a $-$ sign, it is being supplied by the element. But how do we know when the power has a negative or a positive sign?

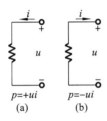

Fig. 1.4 Reference polarities for power using the passive sign convention

(a) Absorbing power
(b) Supplying power

Current direction and voltage polarity play a major role in determining the sign of power. It is therefore important that we pay attention to the relationship between current i and voltage u in Fig. 1.4(a). The voltage polarity and current direction must conform with those shown in Fig. 1.4 (a) in order for the power to have a positive sign. This is known as the *passive sign convention*. By the passive sign convention, current enters through the positive polarity of the voltage. In this case, $p=+ui$ or $ui>0$ implies that the element is absorbing power. However, if $p=-ui$ or $ui<0$, as in Fig. 1.4(b), the element is releasing or supplying power.

In fact, the *law of conservation of energy* must be obeyed in any electric circuit. For this reason, the algebraic sum of power in a circuit, at any instant of time, must be zero:

$$\sum p = 0 \quad (1.8)$$

This again confirms the fact that the total power supplied to the circuit must balance the total power absorbed.

From Eq. (1.6), the energy absorbed or supplied by an element from time t_0 to time t is

$$w = \int_{t_0}^{t} p\,\mathrm{d}t = \int_{t_0}^{t} ui\,\mathrm{d}t \tag{1.9}$$

Energy is the capacity to do work, measured in joules.

The electric power utility companies measure energy in watt-hours (Wh), where

$$1\text{ Wh} = 3600\text{ J}$$

1.5 Summary

① An electric circuit consists of electrical elements connected together.

② Current is the rate of charge flow.

$$i = \frac{\mathrm{d}q}{\mathrm{d}t}$$

③ Voltage is the energy required to move 1C of charge through an element.

$$u = \frac{\mathrm{d}w}{\mathrm{d}q}$$

④ Power is the energy supplied or absorbed per unit time. It is also the product of voltage and current.

$$p = \frac{\mathrm{d}w}{\mathrm{d}t} = ui$$

⑤ According to the passive sign convention, power assumes a positive sign when the current enters the positive polarity of the voltage across an element.

New Words and Expressions

1. electromagnetic   *adj.* 电磁的
2. fundamental   *adj.* 基本的
3. topology   *n.* 拓扑,拓扑学
4. commence   *v.* 着手,开始
5. underlying   *adj.* 根本的,潜在的
6. shock   *n.* 打击
7. coulomb   *n.* 库仑
8. conventional   *adj.* 惯例的
9. with respect to   关于,至于
10. expend   *v.* 消耗,花费
11. instantaneous   *adj.* 瞬间的,即时的
12. deliver   *v.* 释放
13. conform with   符合,与……一致
14. algebraic   *adj.* 代数的
15. instant   *n.* 瞬间,片刻
16. confirm   *v.* 确认,确定

Notes

1. Circuit theory is also valuable to students specializing in other branches of the physical sciences because circuits are a good model for the study of energy systems in

general, and because of the applied mathematics, physics, and topology involved.

电路理论对专门研究自然科学其他学科的学生也十分有用,因为电路一般可很好地作为能量系统研究的模型,并且电路理论涉及应用数学、物理学和拓扑学的相关知识。

2. Charge is an electrical property of the atomic particles of which matter consists, measured in coulombs (C).

电荷是组成物质的原子微粒所具有的电气属性,其量纲为库仑。

3. The common term *signal* is used for an electric quantity such as a current or a voltage when it is used for conveying information.

当像电流或电压这样的电量用于传递信息时,常称这个电量为信号。

Exercises

I. Translate the phrases into English.

1. 电路 2. 电气工程 3. 电机 4. 自然科学 5. 电气设备
6. 电气元件 7. 正电荷 8. 负电荷 9. 直流 10. 交流
11. 电压 12. 导体 13. 功 14. 电动势 15. 电势差
16. 功率 17. 极性 18. 能量守恒定律

II. Answer the following questions according to the text.

1. What is the most basic quantity in an electric circuit?
2. What is the feature of electric charge or electricity?
3. How is electric current created?
4. What is a DC?
5. What is an AC?
6. How does power transmit if the power has a + sign?

III. Translate the sentences into Chinese.

1. An electric circuit is an interconnection of electrical elements.
2. Electric current is the time rate of change of charge.
3. Voltage (or potential difference) is the energy required to move a unit charge through an element, measured in volts.
4. Power is the time rate of expending or absorbing energy, measured in watts.
5. The power absorbed or supplied by an element is the product of the voltage across the element and the current through it.
6. Energy is the capacity to do work, measured in joules.
7. The total power supplied to the circuit must balance the total power absorbed.

Part 2

Basic Laws of Electric Circuit

2.1 Introduction

Part 1 introduced basic concepts such as current, voltage, and power in an electric circuit. To actually determine the values of these variables in a given circuit requires that we understand some fundamental laws that govern electric circuits. These laws, known as Ohm's law and Kirchhoff's laws, form the foundation upon which electric circuit analysis is built[1].

2.2 Ohm's Law

Materials in general have a characteristic behavior of resisting the flow of electric charge. This physical property, or ability to resist current, is known as *resistance* and is represented by the symbol R. The resistance of any material with a uniform cross-sectional area A depends on A and its length l, as shown in Fig. 2.1(a). We can represent resistance (as measured in the laboratory), in mathematical form,

$$R = \rho \frac{l}{A} \quad (2.1)$$

where ρ is known as the *resistivity* of the material in ohm-meters. Good conductors, such as copper and aluminum, have low resistivities, while insulators, such as mica and paper, have high resistivities. The resistivity of semiconductors, such as carbon and silicon, is between those of conductors and insulators.

The circuit element used to model the current-resisting behavior of a material is the *resistor*. For the purpose of constructing a circuit, resistors are usually made from metallic alloys and carbon compounds. The circuit symbol for the resistor is shown in Fig. 2.1(b), where R stands for the resistance of the resistor. The resistor is the simplest passive element.

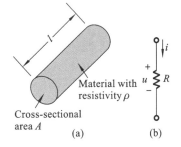

Fig. 2.1 Diagrams of:
(a) Resistor
(b) Circuit symbol for resistance

Georg Simon Ohm (1787-1854), a German physicist, is credited with finding the relationship between current and voltage for a resistor[2]. This relationship is known as *Ohm's law*.

Ohm's law states that the voltage u across a resistor is directly proportional to the current i flowing through the resistor.
That is,

$$u \propto i \tag{2.2}$$

Ohm defined the constant of proportionality for a resistor to be the resistance, R. (The resistance is a material property which can change if the internal or external conditions of the element are altered, e.g., if there are changes in the temperature.) Thus, Eq. (2.2) becomes

$$u = iR \tag{2.3}$$

which is the mathematical form of Ohm's law. R in Eq. (2.3) is measured in the unit of ohms, designated Ω. Thus, the resistance R of an element denotes its ability to resist the flow of electric current; it is measured in ohms (Ω).

We may deduce from Eq. (2.3) that

$$R = \frac{u}{i} \tag{2.4}$$

so that

$$1\Omega = 1 \text{ V/A}$$

To apply Ohm's law as stated in Eq. (2.3), we must pay careful attention to the current direction and voltage polarity. The direction of current i and the polarity of voltage u must conform with the passive sign convention, as shown in Fig. 2.1(b). This implies that current flows from a higher potential to a lower potential in order for $u = iR$. If current flows from a lower potential to a higher potential, $u = -iR$.

The reciprocal of resistance R is named as conductance G.

Since the value of R can range from zero to infinity, it is important that we consider the two extreme possible values of R. An element with $R = 0$ is called a *short circuit*, as shown in Fig. 2.2(a). For a short circuit,

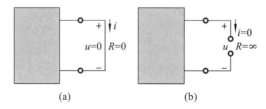

Fig. 2.2 An element with:
(a) Short circuit ($R = 0$) (b) Open circuit ($R = \infty$)

$$u = iR = 0 \tag{2.5}$$

showing that the voltage is zero but the current could be anything. In practice, a short circuit is usually a connecting wire assumed to be a prefect conductor. Thus, a short circuit is a circuit element with resistance approaching zero.

Similarly, an element with $R=\infty$ is known as an *open circuit*, as shown in Fig. 2. 2 (b). For an open circuit,

$$i = \lim_{R \to \infty} \frac{u}{R} = 0 \tag{2.6}$$

indicating that the current is zero, though the voltage could be anything. Thus, an open circuit is a circuit element with resistance approaching infinity.

It should be pointed out that not all resistors obey Ohm's law. A resistor that obeys Ohm's law is known as a *linear* resistor. It has a constant resistance and thus its current-voltage characteristic is as illustrated in Fig. 2. 3(a): Its i-u graph is a straight line passing through the origin. A *nonlinear* resistor does not obey Ohm's law. Its resistance varies with current and its i-u characteristic is typically shown in Fig. 2. 3(b). Examples of devices with nonlinear resistance are the light bulb and the diode. Although all practical resistors may exhibit nonlinear behavior under certain conditions, we will assume in general that all elements actually designated as resistors are linear.

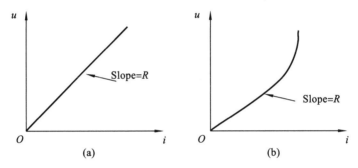

Fig. 2. 3 The i-u characteristic

(a) A linear resistor (b) A nonlinear resistor

The power dissipated by a resistor can be expressed in terms of R. Using Eqs. (1.7) and (2.3),

$$p = ui = i^2 R = \frac{u^2}{R} \tag{2.7}$$

We should note two things from Eq. (2.7):

① The power dissipated in a resistor is a nonlinear function of either current or voltage.

② Since R is positive quantity, the power dissipated in a resistor is always positive. Thus, a resistor always absorbs power from the circuit. This confirms the idea that a resistor is a passive element, incapable of generating energy.

2.3 Kirchhoff's Laws

Ohm's law by itself is not sufficient to analyze circuits. However, when it is coupled with Kirchhoff's two laws, we have a sufficient, powerful set of tools for analyzing a large variety of electric circuits. Kirchhoff's laws were first introduced in 1847 by the German physicist Gustav Robert Kirchhoff (1824-1887). These laws are formally known as Kirchhoff's current law (KCL) and Kirchhoff's voltage law (KVL).

Kirchhoff's first law is based on the law of conservation of charge, which requires that the algebraic sum of charges within a system cannot change.

Kirchhoff's current law (KCL) states that the algebraic sum of currents entering a node (or a closed boundary) is zero.

Mathematically, KCL implies that

$$\sum_{n=1}^{N} i_n = 0 \qquad (2.8)$$

where N is the number of branches connected to the node and i_n is the nth current entering (or leaving) the node. By this law, currents entering a node may be regarded as positive, while currents leaving the node may be taken as negative or vice versa.

An alternative form of KCL is: The sum of the currents entering a node is equal to the sum of the currents leaving the node.

Note that KCL can also be applied to a closed boundary. This may be regarded as a generalized case, because a node may be regarded as a closed surface shrunk to a point. In two dimensions, a closed boundary is the same as a closed path.

A simple application of KCL is combining current sources in parallel. The combined current is the algebraic sum of the current supplied by the individual sources.

Kirchhoff's second law is based on the principle of conservation of energy.

Kirchhoff's voltage law (KVL) states that the algebraic sum of all voltages around a closed path (or loop) is zero.

Expressed mathematically, KVL states that

$$\sum_{m=1}^{M} u_m = 0 \qquad (2.9)$$

where M is the number of voltages in the loop (or the number of branches in the loop) and u_m is the mth voltage.

An alternative form of KVL is: Sum of voltage drops=Sum of voltage rises.

When voltage sources are connected in series, KVL can be applied to obtain the total voltage. The combined voltage is the algebraic sum of the voltage of the individual sources.

2.4　Series Resistors and Voltage Division

The need to combine resistors in series or in parallel occurs so frequently that it warrants special attention. The process of combining the resistors is facilitated by combining two of them at a time. With this in mind, consider the single-loop circuit of Fig.

2.4. The two resistors are in series, since the same current i flows in both of them. Applying Ohm's law to each of the resistors, we obtain

$$u_1 = iR_1, \quad u_2 = iR_2 \quad (2.10)$$

If we apply KVL to the loop (moving in the clockwise direction), we have

$$-u + u_1 + u_2 = 0 \quad (2.11)$$

Combining Eqs. (2.10) and (2.11), we get

$$u = u_1 + u_2 = i(R_1 + R_2) \quad (2.12)$$

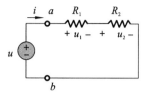

Fig. 2.4 A single-loop circuit with two resistors in series

or

$$i = \frac{u}{R_1 + R_2} \quad (2.13)$$

Notice that Eq. (2.12) can be written as

$$u = iR_{eq} \quad (2.14)$$

Implying that the two resistors can be replaced by an equivalent resistor R_{eq}; that is,

$$R_{eq} = R_1 + R_2 \quad (2.15)$$

In general, the equivalent resistance of any number of resistors connected in series is the sum of the individual resistances.

For N resistors in series then,

$$R_{eq} = R_1 + R_2 + \cdots + R_N = \sum_{n=1}^{N} R_n \quad (2.16)$$

To determine the voltage across each resistor in Fig. 2.4, we substitute Eq. (2.12) into Eq. (2.10) and obtain

$$u_1 = \frac{R_1}{R_1 + R_2} u, \quad u_2 = \frac{R_2}{R_1 + R_2} u \quad (2.17)$$

Notice that the source voltage u is divided among the resistors in direct proportion to their resistances; the larger the resistance, the larger the voltage drop. This is called the *principle of voltage division*, and the circuit in Fig. 2.4 is called a *voltage divider*. In general, if a voltage divider has N resistors ($R_1, R_2, \cdots, R_N$) in series with the source voltage u, the nth resistor (R_n) will have a voltage drop of

$$u_n = \frac{R_n}{R_1 + R_2 + \cdots + R_N} u \quad (2.18)$$

2.5 Parallel Resistors and Current Division

When N resistors are in parallel, as shown in Fig. 2.5, their equivalent resistance R_{eq} and equivalent conductance G_{eq} are

$$\frac{1}{R_{eq}} = \frac{1}{R_1} + \frac{1}{R_2} + \cdots + \frac{1}{R_N} \quad (2.19)$$

$$G_{eq} = G_1 + G_2 + \cdots + G_N \quad (2.20)$$

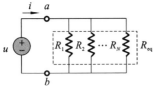

Fig. 2.5 **N resistors in parallel**

If N conductors (G_1, G_2, ⋯, G_N) are in parallel with the source current i, the nth conductor (G_n) will have current

$$i_n = \frac{G_n}{G_1 + G_2 + \cdots + G_N} i \qquad (2.21)$$

This is known as the *principle of current division*.

In general, it is often convenient and possible to combine resistors in series and parallel and reduce a resistive network to a single *equivalent resistance* R_{eq}. Such an equivalent resistance is the resistance between the designated terminals of the network and must exhibit the same i-u characteristics as the original network at the terminals[3].

2.6 Summary

① A resistor is a passive element in which the voltage u across it is directly proportional to[4] the current i through it. That is, a resistor is a device that obeys Ohm's law,

$$u = iR$$

where R is the resistance of the resistor.

② A short circuit is a resistor (a perfectly conducting wire) with zero resistance ($R = 0$). An open circuit is a resistor with infinite resistance ($R = \infty$).

③ The conductance G of a resistor is the reciprocal of its resistance:

$$G = \frac{1}{R}$$

④ Kirchhoff's current law (KCL) states that the currents at any node algebraically sum to zero. In other words, the sum of the currents entering a node equals the sum of currents leaving the node.

⑤ Kirchhoff's voltage law (KVL) states that the voltages around a closed path algebraically sum to zero. In other words, the sum of voltage rises equals the sum of voltage drops.

⑥ Two elements are in series when they are connected sequentially, end to end. When elements are in series, the same current flows through them ($i_1 = i_2$). They are in parallel if they are connected to the same two nodes. Elements in parallel always have the same voltage across them ($u_1 = u_2$).

⑦ When two resistors $R_1 (= 1/G_1)$ and $R_2 (= 1/G_2)$ are in series, their equivalent resistance R_{eq} and equivalent conductance G_{eq} are

$$R_{eq} = R_1 + R_2, \quad G_{eq} = \frac{G_1 G_2}{G_1 + G_2}$$

⑧ When two resistors $R_1 (= 1/G_1)$ and $R_2 (= 1/G_2)$ are in parallel, their equivalent resistance R_{eq} and equivalent conductance G_{eq} are

$$R_{eq} = \frac{R_1 R_2}{R_1 + R_2}, \quad G_{eq} = G_1 + G_2$$

⑨ The voltage division principle for two resistors in series is

$$u_1 = \frac{R_1}{R_1 + R_2} u, \quad u_2 = \frac{R_2}{R_1 + R_2} u$$

⑩ The current division principle for two resistors in parallel is

$$i_1 = \frac{R_2}{R_1 + R_2} i, \quad i_2 = \frac{R_1}{R_1 + R_2} i$$

New Words and Expressions

1. resistance *n.* 电阻
2. uniform *adj.* 一致的,统一的
3. cross-sectional *adj.* 横截面的
4. aluminum *n.* 铝
5. mica *n.* 云母
6. alloy *n.* 合金
7. proportionality *n.* 比例
8. designate *v.* 指定,标出
9. denote *v.* 表示,指示
10. deduce *v.* 推断,演绎出
11. in order for 为了,以便
12. reciprocal *n.* 倒数
13. conductance *n.* 电导
14. diode *n.* 二极管
15. slope *n.* 斜率
16. in terms of 依据,按照
17. be coupled with 与……结合
18. Gustav Robert 古斯塔夫·罗伯特
19. series *n.* 串联,级数
20. parallel *n.* 并联,平行线
21. in direct proportion to 成正比
22. sequentially *adv.* 继续地,循序地
23. end to end 首尾相连

Notes

1. These laws, known as Ohm's law and Kirchhoff's laws, form the foundation upon which electric circuit analysis is built.

(be) known as   以……知名；被认为是；称为

欧姆定律和基尔霍夫定律构成了电路理论的基础,电路分析就建立在这些定律的基础之上。

2. Georg Simon Ohm (1787-1854), a German physicist, is credited with finding the relationship between current and voltage for a resistor.

格奥尔格·西蒙·欧姆(1789-1854),德国物理学家,因其提出了电阻中电流和电压的关系而享誉世界。

3. Such an equivalent resistance is the resistance between the designated terminals of the network and must exhibit the same *i-u* characteristics as the original network at the

terminals.

这样的一个电阻在网络的指定两端等效，并且在这两端等效的电阻具有与原网络相同的伏安特性。

4. be directly proportional to 与 in direct proportion to 的含义相同。

Exercises

I. Translate the phrases into English.

1. 变量　　2. 电阻　　3. 电阻率　　4. 绝缘体　　5. 电阻器
6. 无源元件　7. 常数　　8. 电导　　9. 短路　　10. 开路
11. 线性的　12. 串联　　13. 并联　　14. 电压降　15. 等效电阻

II. Answer the following questions according to the text.

1. What does Ohm's law state?
2. What is a short circuit?
3. What is an open circuit?
4. What is a linear resistor?
5. Why is a resistor a passive element?
6. Can KCL be applied to a closed boundary? Why?
7. What are the elements in series?
8. What are the elements in parallel?

III. Translate the sentences into Chinese.

1. The resistance R of an element denotes its ability to resist the flow of electric current; it is measured in ohms （Ω）.

2. Kirchhoff's current law (KCL) states that the algebraic sum of currents entering a node (or a closed boundary) is zero.

3. If current sources are in parallel, the combined current is the algebraic sum of the current supplied by the individual sources.

4. Kirchhoff's voltage law (KVL) states that the algebraic sum of all voltages around a closed path (or loop) is zero.

5. When voltage sources are connected in series, KVL can be applied to obtain the total voltage. The combined voltage is the algebraic sum of the voltage of the individual sources.

6. The equivalent resistance of any number of resistors connected in series is the sum of the individual resistances.

Part 3

Capacitors and Inductors

3.1 Introduction

In this part, we shall introduce two new and important passive linear circuit elements: the capacitor and the inductor. Unlike resistors, which dissipate energy, capacitors and inductors do not dissipate but store energy, which can be retrieved at a later time. For this reason, capacitors and inductors are called *storage* elements.

The application of resistive circuits is quite limited. With the introduction of capacitors and inductors in this part, we will be able to analyze more important and practical circuits.

We begin by introducing capacitors and describing how to combine them in series or in parallel. Later, we do the same for inductors.

3.2 Capacitors

A capacitor is a passive element designed to store energy in its electric field. Besides resistors, capacitors are the most common electrical components. Capacitors are used extensively in electronics, communications, computers, and power systems. For example, they are used in the tuning circuits of radio receivers and as dynamic memory elements in computer systems.

A capacitor is typically constructed as depicted in Fig. 3.1.

A capacitor consists of two conducting plates separated by an insulator (or dielectric). In many practical applications, the plates may be aluminum foil while the dielectric may be air, ceramic, paper, or mica.

When a voltage source u is connected to the capacitor, as in Fig. 3.2, the source deposits a positive charge q on one plate and a negative charge $-q$ on the other. The capacitor is said to store the electric charge. The amount of charge stored, represented by q, is directly proportional to the applied voltage u, so that

$$q = Cu \qquad (3.1)$$

where C, the constant of proportionality, is known as the *capacitance* of the capacitor. The unit of capacitance is the farad (F), in honor of the English physicist Michael Faraday (1791-1867)[1]. From Eq. (3.1), we may derive the following definition.

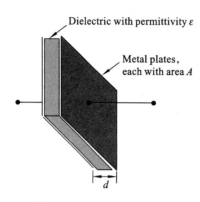   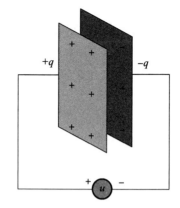

Fig. 3.1 A typical capacitor   Fig. 3.2 A capacitor with applied voltage u

Capacitance is the ratio of the charge on one plate of a capacitor to the voltage difference between the two plates, measured in farads. Note from Eq. (3.1) that 1 farad = 1 coulomb/volt.

Although the capacitance C of a capacitor is the ratio of the charge q per plate to the applied voltage u, it does not depend on q or u. It depends on the physical dimensions of the capacitor. For example, for the parallel-plate capacitor shown in Fig. 3.1, the capacitance is given by

$$C = \frac{\varepsilon A}{d} \tag{3.2}$$

where A is the surface area of each plate, d is the distance between the plates, and ε is the permittivity of the dielectric material between the plates.

Capacitors are commercially available in different values and types. Typically, capacitors have values in the picofarad (pF) to microfarad (μF) range. They are described by the dielectric material they are made of and by whether they are of fixed or variable type. Figure 3.3 shows the circuit symbols for fixed and variable capacitors. Note that according to the passive sign convention, current is considered to flow into the positive terminal of the capacitor when the capacitor is being charged, and out of the positive terminal when the capacitor is discharging.

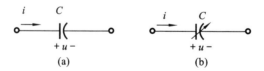

Fig. 3.3 Circuit symbols for capacitors
(a) Fixed capacitor (b) Variable capacitor

To obtain the current-voltage relationship of the capacitor, we take the derivative of both sides of Eq. (3.1). Since

$$i = \frac{dq}{dt} \tag{3.3}$$

differentiating both sides of Eq. (3.1) gives

$$i = C\frac{du}{dt} \tag{3.4}$$

This is the current-voltage relationship for a capacitor, assuming the positive sign convention.

The voltage-current relation of the capacitor can be obtained by integrating both sides of Eq. (3.4). We get

$$u = \frac{1}{C}\int_{-\infty}^{t} i\,dt \tag{3.5}$$

or

$$u = \frac{1}{C}\int_{t_0}^{t} i\,dt + u(t_0) \tag{3.6}$$

where $u(t_0) = q(t_0)/C$ is the voltage across the capacitor at time t_0. Equation (3.6) shows that capacitor voltage depends on the past history of the capacitor current. Hence, the capacitor has memory—a property that is often exploited.

The instantaneous power delivered to the capacitor is

$$p = ui = Cu\frac{du}{dt} \tag{3.7}$$

The energy stored in the capacitor is therefore

$$w = \int_{-\infty}^{t} p\,dt = C\int_{-\infty}^{t} u\frac{du}{dt}dt = C\int_{-\infty}^{t} u\,du = \frac{1}{2}Cu^2 \bigg|_{t=-\infty}^{t} \tag{3.8}$$

We note that $u(-\infty) = 0$, because the capacitor was uncharged at $t = -\infty$. Thus,

$$w = \frac{1}{2}Cu^2 \tag{3.9}$$

Using Eq. (3.1), we may rewrite Eq. (3.9) as

$$w = \frac{q^2}{2C} \tag{3.10}$$

Equation (3.9) or (3.10) represents the energy stored in the electric field that exists between the plates of the capacitor. This energy can be retrieved, since an ideal capacitor cannot dissipate energy. In fact, the word *capacitor* is derived from this element's capacity to store energy in an electric field.

We should note the following important properties of a capacitor:

① Note from Eq. (3.4) that when the voltage across a capacitor is not changing with time (i.e., DC voltage), the current through the capacitor is zero. Thus, a capacitor is an open circuit to DC.

However, if a battery (DC voltage) is connected across a capacitor, the capacitor charges.

② The voltage on the capacitor must be continuous. That is, the voltage on a capacitor cannot change abruptly.

The capacitor resists an abrupt change in the voltage across it. According to Eq. (3.4), a discontinuous change in voltage requires an infinite current, which is physically impossible. Conversely, the current through a capacitor can change instantaneously.

③ The ideal capacitor does not dissipate energy. It takes power from the circuit when storing energy in its field and returns previously stored energy when delivering power to the circuit[2].

④ A real, nonideal capacitor has a parallel-model leakage resistance. The leakage resistance may be as high as 100MΩ and can be neglected for most practical applications. For this reason, we will assume ideal capacitors in this book.

3.3 Inductors

An inductor is a passive element designed to store energy in its magnetic field. Inductors find numerous applications in electronic and power systems. They are used in power supplies, transformers, radios, TVs, radars, and electric motors.

Any conductor of electric current has inductive properties and may be regarded as an inductor. But in order to enhance the inductive effect, a practical inductor is usually formed into a cylindrical coil with many turns of conducting wire[3].

An inductor consists of a coil of conducting wire. If current is allowed to pass through an inductor, it is found that the voltage across the inductor is directly proportional to the time rate of change of the current. Using the passive sign convention,

$$u = L \frac{\mathrm{d}i}{\mathrm{d}t} \tag{3.11}$$

where L is the constant of proportionality called the *inductance* of the inductor. The unit of inductance is the henry (H), named in honor of the American inventor Joseph Henry (1797-1878)[4]. It is clear from Eq. (3.11) that 1 henry equals 1 volt-second per ampere.

Inductance is the property whereby an inductor exhibits opposition to the change of current flowing through it, measured in henrys[5].

Like capacitors, commercially available inductors come in different values and types. Typical practical inductors have inductance values ranging from a few microhenrys (μH), as in communication systems, to tens of henrys as in power systems. The circuit symbols for inductors are shown in Fig. 3.4, following the passive sign convention.

The current-voltage relationship is obtained from Eq. (3.11) as

$$\mathrm{d}i = \frac{1}{L} u \mathrm{d}t$$

Integrating gives

$$i = \frac{1}{L} \int_{-\infty}^{t} u(t) \mathrm{d}t \tag{3.12}$$

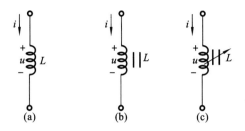

Fig. 3.4 Circuit symbols for inductors

(a) Air-core (b) Iron-core (c) Variable iron-core

or

$$i = \frac{1}{L}\int_{t_0}^{t} u(t)\,\mathrm{d}t + i(t_0) \tag{3.13}$$

where $i(t_0)$ is the total current for $-\infty < t < t_0$ and $i(-\infty) = 0$. The idea of making $i(-\infty) = 0$ is practical and reasonable, because there must be a time in the past when there was no current in the inductor.

The inductor is designed to store energy in its magnetic field. The energy stored can be obtained from Eq. (3.11). The power delivered to the inductor is

$$p = ui = (L\frac{\mathrm{d}i}{\mathrm{d}t})i \tag{3.14}$$

The energy stored is

$$w = \int_{-\infty}^{t} p\,\mathrm{d}t = \int_{-\infty}^{t} (L\frac{\mathrm{d}i}{\mathrm{d}t})i\,\mathrm{d}t = L\int_{-\infty}^{t} i\,\mathrm{d}i = \frac{1}{2}Li^2(t) - \frac{1}{2}Li^2(-\infty) \tag{3.15}$$

Since $i(-\infty) = 0$,

$$w = \frac{1}{2}Li^2 \tag{3.16}$$

We should note the following important properties of an inductor:

① Note from Eq. (3.11) that the voltage across an inductor is zero when the current is constant. Thus, an inductor acts like a short circuit to DC.

② An important property of the inductor is its opposition to the change in current flowing through it.

The current through an inductor cannot change instantaneously.

According to Eq. (3.11), a discontinuous change in the current through an inductor requires an infinite voltage, which is not physically possible. Thus, an inductor opposes an abrupt change in the current through it. However, the voltage across an inductor can change abruptly.

③ Like the ideal capacitor, the ideal inductor does not dissipate energy. The energy stored in it can be retrieved at a later time. The inductor takes power from the circuit when storing energy and delivers power to the circuit when returning previously stored energy.

④ A practical, nonideal inductor has a significant resistive component, as shown in Fig. 3.5. This is due to the fact that the inductor is made of a conducting material such as

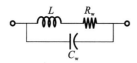

Fig. 3.5 Circuit model for a practical inductor

copper, which has some resistance. This resistance is called the *winding resistance* R_w, and it appears in series with the inductance of the inductor. The presence of R_w makes it both an energy storage device and an energy dissipation device. Since R_w is usually very small, it is ignored in most cases.

The nonideal inductor also has a *winding capacitance* C_w due to the capacitive coupling between the conducting coils. C_w is very small and can be ignored in most cases, except at high frequencies. We will assume ideal inductors in this book.

3.4　Summary

① The current through a capacitor is directly proportional to the time rate of change of the voltage across it.

The current through a capacitor is zero unless the voltage is changing. Thus, a capacitor acts like an open circuit to a DC source.

② The voltage across a capacitor is directly proportional to the time integral of the current through it.

$$u = \frac{1}{C}\int_{-\infty}^{t} i \mathrm{d}t = \frac{1}{C}\int_{t_0}^{t} i \mathrm{d}t + u(t_0)$$

The voltage across a capacitor cannot change instantly.

③ The voltage across an inductor is directly proportional to the time rate of change of the current through it.

$$u = L \frac{\mathrm{d}i}{\mathrm{d}t}$$

The voltage across the inductor is zero unless the current is changing. Thus an inductor acts like a short circuit to a DC source.

④ The current through an inductor is directly proportional to the time integral of the voltage across it.

$$i = \frac{1}{L}\int_{-\infty}^{t} u \mathrm{d}t = \frac{1}{L}\int_{t_0}^{t} u(t) \mathrm{d}t + i(t_0)$$

The current through an inductor cannot change instantly.

⑤ At any given time t, the energy stored in a capacitor is $\frac{1}{2}Cu^2$, while the energy stored in an inductor is $\frac{1}{2}Li^2$.

New Words and Expressions

1. capacitor　*n.* 电容器
2. inductor　*n.* 电感器,感应器

3. retrieve   *v.* 恢复,重新得到
4. tuning   *n.* 调谐,调音
5. dynamic   *adj.* 动态的,动力的
6. depict   *v.* 描述,描画
7. dielectric   *n.* 电介质,绝缘体
8. foil   *n.* 箔,金属薄片
9. ceramic   *n.* 陶瓷
10. deposit   *v.* 存放,使沉积
11. capacitance   *n.* 电容
12. dimension   *n.* 尺寸,维
13. permittivity   *n.* 介电常数
14. derivative   *n.* 导数
15. differentiate   *v.* 求微分,区分
16. integrate   *v.* 求……的积分
17. exploit   *v.* 开发,开拓
18. abruptly   *adv.* 突然地
19. conversely   *adv.* 相反地
20. leakage resistance   漏泄电阻
21. power supply   电源
22. cylindrical   *adj.* 圆柱形的
23. coil   *n.* 线圈,卷
24. winding   *n.* 绕组,线圈

Notes

1. The unit of capacitance is the farad (F), in honor of the English physicist Michael Faraday (1791-1867).

in honor of   向……表示敬意

电容的量纲是法拉(F),以纪念英国物理学家迈克尔·法拉第(1791—1867)。

2. It takes power from the circuit when storing energy in its field and returns previously stored energy when delivering power to the circuit.

当电容在电场中储能时,它从电路吸收功率;当电容向电路提供功率时,它就释放先前储存的能量。

3. But in order to enhance the inductive effect, a practical inductor is usually formed into a cylindrical coil with many turns of conducting wire.

为了增加电感的感应作用,实际的电感通常是由许多匝导线绕制成的圆柱形线圈构成的。

4. The unit of inductance is the henry (H), named in honor of the American inventor Joseph Henry (1797-1878).

Joseph Henry   约瑟夫·亨利(1797—1878),美国发明家。

电感的量纲是亨(H),是为纪念美国发明家约瑟夫·亨利(1797—1878)而命名的。

5. Inductance is the property whereby an inductor exhibits opposition to the change of current flowing through it, measured in henrys.

whereby   *adv.* 由此,借此

电感器具有与流经它的电流变化相反的特性,用电感来描述这一特性,其量纲为亨利。

Exercises

I. Translate the phrases into English.

1. 电容器　　2. 电感器　　3. 储能元件　　4. 电场　　5. 充电
6. 放电　　　7. 动态的　　8. 电介质　　　9. 电容　　10. 磁场
11. 电源　　 12. 变压器　 13. 电机　　　 14. 线圈　 15. 电感
16. 导线　　 17. 绕组　　 18. 漏电阻

II. Answer the following questions according to the text.

1. Why are capacitors and inductors called storage elements?
2. According to the passive sign convention, how does current flow when the capacitor being charged?
3. Why can the capacitor have memory?
4. Why is a capacitor an open circuit to DC?
5. Why does an inductor act like a short circuit to DC?

III. Translate the sentences into Chinese.

1. Capacitance is the ratio of the charge on one plate of a capacitor to the voltage difference between the two plates, measured in farads.
2. The voltage on a capacitor cannot change abruptly.
3. If current is allowed to pass through an inductor, it is found that the voltage across the inductor is directly proportional to the time rate of change of the current.
4. The idea of making $i(-\infty)=0$ is practical and reasonable, because there must be a time in the past when there was no current in the inductor.
5. An important property of the inductor is its opposition to the change in current flowing through it.

Part 4

Computers

4.1 Introduction

Computers have led to a third revolution for civilization, with the information revolution taking its place alongside the agricultural and the industrial revolutions. The resulting multiplication of humankind's intellectual strength and reach naturally has affected our everyday life profoundly and changed the ways in which the search for new knowledge is carried out[1]. There is now a new vein of scientific investigation, with computational scientist jointing theoretical and experimental scientists in the exploration of new frontiers in astronomy, biology, chemistry, and physics, among others.

The computer revolution continues. Each time the cost of computing improves by another factor of 10, the opportunities for computers multiply. Applications that were economically infeasible suddenly become practical. In the recent past, the following applications were "computer science fiction".

- *Computers in automobiles*: Until microprocessors improved dramatically in price and performance in the early 1980s, computer control of cars was ludicrous. Today, computers reduce pollution, improve fuel efficiency via engine controls, and increase safety through blind spot warnings, lane departure warnings, moving object detection, and air bag inflation to protect occupants in a crash.
- *Cell phones*: Who would have dreamed that advances in computer systems would lead to more than half of the planet having mobile phones, allowing person-to-person communication to almost anyone anywhere in the world?
- *Search engines*: As the content of the web grew in size and in value, finding relevant information became increasingly important. Today, many people rely on search engines for such a large part of their lives that it would be a hardship to go without them.

Clearly, advances in this technology now affect almost every aspect of our society. Hardware advances have allowed programmers to create wonderfully useful software, which explains why computers are omnipresent.

4.2 Computer Function

The functioning of a computer is, in essence, simple. Figure 4.1 depicts the basic functions that a computer can perform. In general terms, there are only four:

- Data processing;
- Data storage;
- Data movement;
- Control.

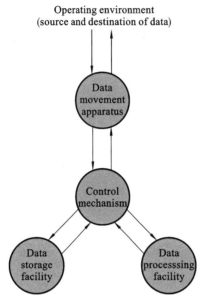

Fig. 4.1 A functional view of the computer

The computer, of course, must be able to process data. The data may take a wide variety of forms, and the range of processing requirements is broad.

It is also essential that a computer *store data*. Even if the computer is processing data on the fly (i. e., data come in and get processed, and the results go out immediately), the computer must temporarily store at least those pieces of data that are being worked on at any given moment. Thus, there is at least a short-term data storage function. Equally important, the computer performs a long-term data storage function. Files of data are stored on the computer for subsequent retrieval and update.

The computer must be able to *move data* between itself and the outside world. The computer's operating environment consists of devices that serve as either sources or destinations of data. When data are received from or delivered to a device that is directly connected to the computer, the process is known as *input-output* (I/O), and the device is referred to as a *peripheral*. When data are moved over longer distances, to or from a remote device, the process is known as *data communications*.

Finally, there must be *control* of these three functions. Ultimately, this control is exercised by the individual who provides the computer with instructions. Within the computer, a control unit manages the computer's resources and orchestrates the performance of its functional parts in response to those instructions.

4.3 Computer Structure

A computer is a complex system; contemporary computers contain millions of elementary electronic components. The computer interacts in some fashion with its external environment. In general, all of its linkages to the external environment can be classified as peripheral devices or communication lines.

But of greater concern here is the internal structure of the computer itself, which is shown in Fig. 4.2. There are four main structural components.

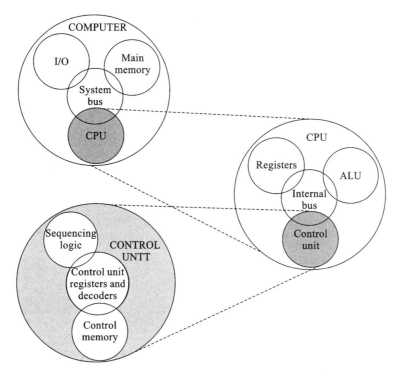

Fig. 4.2 The computer: top-level structure

• *Central processing unit* (*CPU*): Controls the operation of the computer and performs its data processing functions; often simply referred to as the processor.
• *Main memory*: Stores data.
• *I/O*: Moves data between the computer and its external environment.
• *System interconnection*: Some mechanism that provides for communication among CPU, main memory, and I/O. A common example of system interconnection is by means of a *system bus*, consisting of a number of conducting wires to which all the other components attach.

There may be one or more of each of the aforementioned components. Traditionally, there has been just a single processor. In recent years, there has been increasing use of multiple processors in a single computer. The most interesting and in some ways the most complex component is the CPU. Its major structural components are as follows:

• *Control unit*: Controls the operation of the CPU and hence the computer.
• *Arithmetic and logic unit* (*ALU*): Performs the computer's data processing functions.
• *Registers*: Provide storage internal to the CPU.
• *CPU interconnection*: Some mechanism that provides for communication among the control unit, ALU, and registers.

Virtually all contemporary computer designs are based on concepts developed by John von Neumann at the Institute for Advanced Studies, Princeton[2]. Such a design is referred to as the von Neumann architecture and is based on three key concepts:

- Data and instructions are stored in a single read-write memory.
- The contents of this memory are addressable by location, without regard to the type of data contained there.
- Execution occurs in a sequential fashion (unless explicitly modified) from one instruction to the next[3].

There is a small set of basic logic components that can be combined in various ways to store binary data and perform arithmetic and logical operations on that data. If there is a particular computation to be performed, a configuration of logic components designed specifically for that computation could be constructed[4]. We can think of the process of connecting the various components in the desired configuration as a form of programming. The resulting "program" is in the form of hardware and is termed a *hardwired program*.

Programming is now much easier. Instead of rewiring the hardware for each new program, all we need to do is provide a new sequence of codes. Each code is, in effect, an instruction, and part of the hardware interprets each instruction and generates control signals. To distinguish this new method of programming, a sequence of codes or instructions is called *software*.

Figure 4.3 illustrates these top-level components and suggests the interactions among them. The CPU exchanges data with memory. For this purpose, it typically makes use of two internal (to the CPU) registers: a *memory address register* (MAR), which specifies the address in memory for the next read or write, and a *memory buffer register* (MBR), which contains the data to be written into memory or receives the data read from memory. Similarly, an *I/O address register* (I/O AR) specifies a particular I/O device. An *I/O buffer register* (I/O BR) is used for the exchange of data between an I/O module and the CPU.

A memory module consists of a set of locations, defined by sequentially numbered addresses. Each location contains a binary number that can be interpreted as either an instruction or data. An I/O module transfers data from external devices to CPU and memory, and vice versa. It contains internal buffers for temporarily holding these data until they can be sent on.

4.4 Classes of Computing Applications

Although a common set of hardware technologies is used in computers ranging from smart home appliances to cell phones to the largest supercomputers, these different applications have different design requirements and employ the core hardware technologies

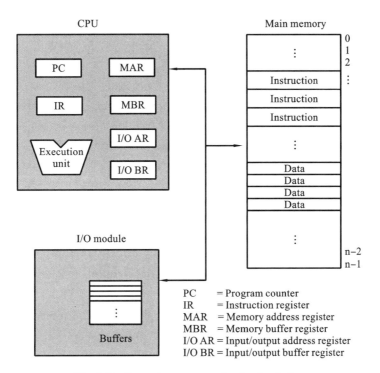

Fig. 4.3 Computer components: top-level view

in different ways. Broadly speaking, computers are used in three different classes of applications.

Personal computers (*PCs*) are possibly the best known form of computing, which readers of this part have likely used extensively. Personal computers emphasize delivery of good performance to single users at a low cost and usually execute third-party software. This class of computing drove the evolution of many computing technologies.

Servers are the modern form of what were once much larger computers, and are usually accessed only via a network. Servers are oriented to carrying large workloads, which may consist of either single complex applications—usually a scientific or engineering application—or handling many small jobs, such as would occur in building a large web server. These applications are usually based on software from another source (such as a database or simulation system), but are often modified or customized for a particular function. Servers are built from the same basic technology as desktop computers, but provide for greater computing, storage, and input/output capacity. In general, servers also place a greater emphasis on dependability, since a crash is usually more costly than it would be on a single-user PC.

Servers span the widest range in cost and capability. At the low end, a server may be little more than a desktop computer without a screen or keyboard and cost a thousand dollars. These low-end servers are typically used for file storage, small business applications, or simple web serving. At the other extreme are supercomputers, which at the present consist of tens of thousands of processors and many terabytes of memory, and cost tens to hundreds of millions of dollars. Supercomputers are usually used for high-end scientific and engineering calculations, such as weather forecasting, oil exploration, protein structure determination, and other large-scale problems. Although such supercomputers represent the peak of computing capability, they represent a relatively small fraction of the servers and a relatively small fraction of the overall computer market in terms of total revenue.

Embedded computers are the largest class of computers and span the widest range of applications and performance. Embedded computers include the microprocessors found in your car, the computers in a television set, and the networks of processors that control a modern airplane or cargo ship. Embedded computing systems are designed to run one application or one set of related applications that are normally integrated with the hardware and delivered as a single system; thus, despite the large number of embedded computers, most users never really see that they are using a computer[5]!

Embedded applications often have unique application requirements that combine a minimum performance with stringent limitations on cost or power. For example, consider a music player: the processor needs only be as fast as necessary to handle its limited function, and beyond that, minimizing cost and power are the most important objectives. Despite their low cost, embedded computers often have lower tolerance for failure, since the results can vary from upsetting (when your new television crashes) to devastating (such as might occur when the computer in a plane or cargo ship crashes). In consumer-oriented embedded applications, such as a digital home appliance, dependability is achieved primarily through simplicity—the emphasis is on doing one function as perfectly as possible. In large embedded systems, techniques of redundancy from the server world are often employed.

New Words and Expressions

1. alongside *prep.* 与……一起
2. multiplication *n.* 增加,乘法
3. intellectual *adj.* 智力的
4. vein *n.* 若干,纹理,风格
5. astronomy *n.* 天文学
6. dramatically *adv.* 显著地
7. ludicrous *adj.* 不合理的
8. departure *n.* 离开,违背
9. occupant *n.* 占用者
10. search engine 搜索引擎
11. omnipresent *adj.* 无所不在的
12. in essence 本质上
13. depict *v.* 描述
14. subsequent *adj.* 随后的
15. retrieval *n.* 恢复
16. peripheral *n.* 外部设备
17. orchestrate *v.* 把……协调地结合起来
18. contemporary *adj.* 当代的
19. aforementioned *adj.* 上述的

20. addressable *adj.* 可寻址的
21. explicitly *adv.* 明确地
22. sequentially *adv.* 循序地
23. span *v.* 跨越，持续
24. terabyte *n.* 太字节，万亿字节
25. stringent *adj.* 严格的
26. redundancy *n.* 冗余

Notes

1. The resulting multiplication of humankind's intellectual strength and reach naturally has affected our everyday life profoundly and changed the ways in which the search for new knowledge is carried out.

由此产生的人类智力的力量和触角的倍增，深刻地影响了人们的日常生活，并改变了人们探索新知识的方式。

2. Virtually all contemporary computer designs are based on concepts developed by John von Neumann at the Institute for Advanced Studies, Princeton.

John von Neumann 约翰·冯·诺依曼(1903—1957)，美籍匈牙利数学家，首先提出了计算机体系结构(即冯·诺依曼体系结构)的设想，被后人称为"数字计算机之父"。

几乎所有现代计算机的设计都遵循普林斯顿高等研究院的约翰·冯·诺依曼提出的概念。

3. Execution occurs in a sequential fashion (unless explicitly modified) from one instruction to the next.

程序(除非明显修改过)从一条指令到下一条指令按顺序执行。

4. If there is a particular computation to be performed, a configuration of logic components designed specifically for that computation could be constructed.

如果要执行特定的计算，需要对为该计算专门设计的逻辑组件进行配置。

5. Embedded computing systems are designed to run one application or one set of related applications that are normally integrated with the hardware and delivered as a single system; thus, despite the large number of embedded computers, most users never really see that they are using a computer!

嵌入式计算系统是为运行一个或一组通常与硬件集成的相关应用而设计的，并作为单片系统交付；因此，尽管有大量的嵌入式计算机在使用，大多数用户却从来没有真正意识到自己在使用计算机！

Exercises

I. Translate the phrases into English.

1. 计算成本　　2. 微处理器　　3. 搜索引擎　　4. 硬件
5. 软件　　　　6. 程序　　　　7. 数据存储　　8. 外设

9. 通信	10. 指令	11. 控制单元	12. 中央处理单元
13. 系统总线	14. 代码	15. 算术逻辑单元	16. 读写存储器
17. 配置	18. 可寻址的	19. 寄存器	20. 巨型计算机
21. 服务器	22. 数据库	23. 面向用户	24. 译码器

25. 嵌入式计算机

II. Answer the following questions according to the text.

1. What basic functions can a computer perform?

2. How many parts does a computer consist mainly of?

3. What is the software referred to as?

4. Where is the exchange of data between an I/O module and the CPU done?

5. How can the server be accessed?

6. Why do embedded computers have lower tolerance for failure?

III. Translate the sentences into Chinese.

1. Even if the computer is processing data on the fly, the computer must temporarily store at least those pieces of data that are being worked on at any given moment.

2. When data are received from or delivered to a device that is directly connected to the computer, the process is known as *input-output* (I/O), and the device is referred to as a *peripheral*.

3. Within the computer, a control unit manages the computer's resources and orchestrates the performance of its functional parts in response to those instructions.

4. Central processing unit (CPU) controls the operation of the computer and performs its data processing functions; often simply referred to as the processor.

5. A memory module consists of a set of locations, defined by sequentially numbered addresses. Each location contains a binary number that can be interpreted as either an instruction or data.

6. Personal computers emphasize delivery of good performance to single users at a low cost and usually execute third-party software.

7. Servers are built from the same basic technology as desktop computers, but provide for greater computing, storage, and input/output capacity.

Part 5

Operational Amplifiers

5.1 Introduction

We are now ready to study an active circuit element of paramount importance: the *operational amplifier*, or *op amp* for short. The op amp is a versatile circuit building block.

The op amp is an electronic unit that behaves like a voltage-controlled voltage source. It can also be used in making a voltage- or current-controlled current source. An op amp can sum signals, amplify a signal, integrate it, or differentiate it. The ability of the op amp to perform these mathematical operations is the reason it is called an *operational amplifier*. It is also the reason for the widespread use of op amps in analog design. Op amps are popular in practical circuit designs because they are versatile, inexpensive, easy to use, and fun to work with.

5.2 Operational Amplifiers

An operational amplifier is designed so that it performs some mathematical operations when external components, such as resistors and capacitors, are connected to its terminals. Thus, an op amp is an active circuit element designed to perform mathematical operations of addition, subtraction, multiplication, division, differentiation, and integration.

The op amp is an electronic device consisting of a complex arrangement of resistors, transistors, capacitors, and diodes. A full discussion of what is inside the op amp is beyond the scope of this part. It will suffice to treat the op amp as a circuit building block and simply study what takes place at its terminals.

Op amps are commercially available in integrated circuit packages in several forms[1]. A typical op amp is the eight-pin dual in-line package (or DIP), shown in Fig. 5.1(a). Pin or terminal 8 is unused, and terminals 1 and 5 are of little concern to us. The five important terminals are:

- The inverting input, pin 2;
- The noninverting input, pin 3;

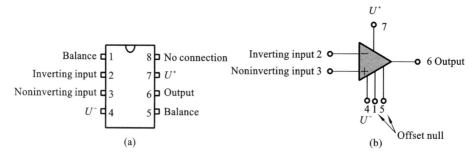

Fig. 5.1 A typical op amp

(a) Pin configuration   (b) Circuit symbol

- The output, pin 6;
- The positive power supply U^+, pin 7;
- The negative power supply U^-, pin 4.

The circuit symbol for the op amp is the triangle in Fig. 5.1(b); as shown, the op amp has two inputs and one output. The inputs are marked with minus (−) and plus (+) to specify *inverting* and *noninverting* inputs, respectively. An input applied to the noninverting terminal will appear with the same polarity at the output, while an input applied to the inverting terminal will appear inverted at the output[2].

As an active element, the op amp must be powered by a voltage supply as typically shown in Fig. 5.2. Although the power supplies are often ignored in op amp circuit diagrams for the sake of simplicity, the power supply currents must not be overlooked[3]. By KCL,

$$i_o = i_1 + i_2 + i_+ + i_- \tag{5.1}$$

The equivalent circuit model of an op amp is shown in Fig. 5.3. The output section consists of a voltage-controlled source in series with the output resistance R_o. It is evident from Fig. 5.3 that the input resistance R_i is the Thevenin equivalent resistance[4] seen at the input terminals, while the output resistance R_o is the Thevenin equivalent resistance seen at the output. The differential input voltage u_d is given by

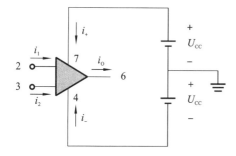

Fig. 5.2 Powering the op amp

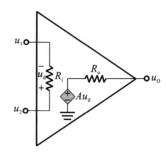

Fig. 5.3 The equivalent circuit of the nonideal op amp

$$u_d = u_2 - u_1 \tag{5.2}$$

where u_1 is the voltage between the inverting terminal and ground and u_2 is the voltage between the noninverting terminal and ground. The op amp senses the difference between the two inputs, multiplies it by the gain A, and causes the resulting voltage to appear at the output. Thus, the output u_o is given by

$$u_o = A u_d = A(u_2 - u_1) \tag{5.3}$$

A is called the *open-loop voltage gain* because it is the gain of the op amp without any external feedback from output to input. Table 5.1 shows typical values of voltage gain A, input resistance R_i, output resistance R_o, and supply voltage U_{CC}.

Table 5.1 Typical ranges for op amp parameters

Parameters	Typical ranges	Ideal values
Open-loop gain, A	10^5 to 10^8	∞
Input resistance, R_i	10^5 to 10^{13} Ω	∞ Ω
Output resistance, R_o	10 to 100 Ω	0 Ω
Supply voltage, U_{CC}	5 to 24 V	

The concept of feedback is crucial to our understanding of op amp circuits. A negative feedback is achieved when the output is fed back to the inverting terminal of the op amp. When there is a feedback path from output to input, the ratio of the output voltage to the input voltage is called the *closed-loop gain*. As a result of the negative feedback, it can be shown that the closed-loop gain is almost insensitive to the open-loop gain A of the op amp. For this reason, op amps are used in circuits with feedback paths.

A practical limitation of the op amp is that the magnitude of its output voltage cannot exceed $|U_{CC}|$. In other words, the output voltage is dependent on and is limited by the power supply voltage. Figure 5.4 illustrates that the op amp can operate in three modes, depending on the differential input voltage u_d:

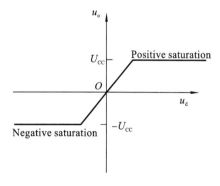

Fig. 5.4 Op amp output voltage u_o as a function of the differential input voltage u_d

- Positive saturation, $u_o = U_{CC}$;

- Linear region, $-U_{CC} \leqslant u_o = Au_d \leqslant U_{CC}$;
- Negative saturation, $u_o = -U_{CC}$.

If we attempt to increase u_d beyond the linear range, the op amp becomes saturated and yields $u_o = U_{CC}$ or $u_o = -U_{CC}$.

5.3 Ideal Op Amp

To facilitate the understanding of op amp circuits, we will assume ideal op amps. An op amp is ideal if it has the following characteristics:
- Infinite open-loop gain, $A \approx \infty$;
- Infinite input resistance, $R_i \approx \infty$;
- Zero output resistance, $R_o \approx 0$.

An ideal op amp is an amplifier with infinite open-loop gain, infinite input resistance, and zero output resistance.

Although assuming an ideal op amp provides only an approximate analysis, most modern amplifiers have such large gains and input impedances that the approximate analysis is a good one. Unless stated otherwise, we will assume from now on that every op amp is ideal.

Two important characteristics of the ideal op amp are:
- The currents into both input terminals are zero:

$$i_1 = 0, \quad i_2 = 0 \qquad (5.4)$$

This is due to infinite input resistance. An infinite resistance between the input terminals implies that an open circuit exists there and current cannot enter the op amp. But the output current is not necessarily zero according to Eq. (5.1).

- The voltage across the input terminals is negligibly small; i.e.,

$$u_d = u_2 - u_1 \approx 0 \qquad (5.5)$$

or

$$u_1 = u_2 \qquad (5.6)$$

Thus, an ideal op amp has zero current into its two input terminals and negligibly small voltage between the two input terminals. Equations (5.4) and (5.6) are extremely important and should be regarded as the key handles to analyzing op amp circuits.

5.4 Inverting Amplifier

In this and the following sections, we consider some useful op amp circuits that often serve as modules for designing more complex circuits. The first of such op amp circuits is the inverting amplifier shown in Fig. 5.5. In this circuit, the noninverting input is grounded, u_i is connected to the inverting input through R_1, and the feedback resistor R_f is connected between the inverting input and output. Our goal is to obtain the relationship between the input voltage u_i and the output voltage u_o. Applying KCL at node 1, but $u_1 = u_2 = 0$ for an ideal op amp, since the noninverting terminal is grounded. Hence,

$$\frac{u_i}{R_1} = -\frac{u_o}{R_f}$$

or

$$u_o = -\frac{R_f}{R_1} u_i \qquad (5.7)$$

The voltage gain is $A_u = u_o/u_i = -R_f/R_1$. The designation of the circuit in Fig. 5.5 as an *inverter* arises from the negative sign. Thus, an inverting amplifier reverses the polarity of the input signal while amplifying it.

Notice that the gain is the feedback resistance divided by the input resistance which means that the gain depends only on the external elements connected to the op amp.

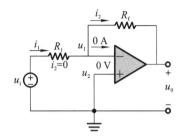

Fig. 5.5 The inverting amplifier

5.5 Noninverting Amplifier

Another important application of the op amp is the noninverting amplifier shown in Fig. 5.6. In this case, the input voltage u_i is applied directly at the noninverting input terminal, and resistor R_1 is connected between the ground and the inverting terminal. We are interested in the output voltage and the voltage gain. Application of KCL at the inverting terminal gives

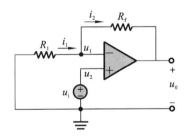

Fig. 5.6 The noninverting amplifier

$$i_1 = i_2 \quad \Rightarrow \quad \frac{0 - u_1}{R_1} = \frac{u_1 - u_o}{R_f} \qquad (5.8)$$

But $u_1 = u_2 = u_i$. Equation (5.8) becomes

$$\frac{-u_i}{R_1} = \frac{u_i - u_o}{R_f}$$

or

$$u_o = (1 + \frac{R_f}{R_1}) u_i \qquad (5.9)$$

The voltage gain is $A_u = u_o/u_i = 1 + R_f/R_1$, which does not have a negative sign. Thus, the output has the same polarity as the input.

A noninverting amplifier is an op amp circuit designed to provide a positive voltage gain.

Again we notice that the gain depends only on the external resistors.

Notice that if feedback resistor $R_f = 0$ (short circuit) or $R_1 = \infty$ (open circuit) or both, the gain becomes 1. Under these conditions ($R_f = 0$ and $R_1 = \infty$), the circuit in Fig. 5.6

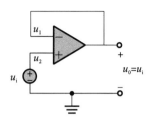

Fig. 5.7 The voltage follower

becomes that shown in Fig. 5.7, which is called a *voltage follower* (or *unity gain amplifier*) because the output follows the input. Thus, for a voltage follower

$$u_o = u_i \qquad (5.10)$$

Such a circuit has a very high input impedance and is therefore useful as an intermediate-stage (or buffer) amplifier to isolate one circuit from another. The voltage follower minimizes interaction between the two stages and eliminates interstage loading.

5.6 Summary

① The op amp is a high-gain amplifier that has high input resistance and low output resistance.

② An ideal op amp has an infinite input resistance, a zero output resistance, and an infinite gain.

③ For an ideal op amp, the current into each of its two input terminals is zero, and the voltage across its input terminals is negligibly small.

④ In an inverting amplifier, the output voltage is a negative multiple of the input.

⑤ In a noninverting amplifier, the output is a positive multiple of the input.

⑥ In a voltage follower, the output follows the input.

New Words and Expressions

1. paramount   *adj.* 最重要的
2. versatile   *adj.* 通用的
3. building block   结构单元,标准元件
4. terminal   *n.* 线接头,终端
5. suffice   *v.* 足够
6. package   *n.* 包,套装软件
7. pin   *n.* 针,插脚
8. offset   *n.* 偏离
9. null   *n.* 空,空字符
10. overlook   *v.* 忽略,不计较
11. for the sake of   为了
12. crucial   *adj.* 重要的,决定性的
13. insensitive   *adj.* 无感觉的
14. saturation   *n.* 饱和
15. yield   *v.* 产出,出产
16. facilitate   *v.* 帮助,促进
17. extremely   *adv.* 非常,极端地
18. handle   *n.* 理解,明白
19. module   *n.* 模块
20. designation   *n.* 名称,指定,指示
21. intermediate   *adj.* 中间的,中级的

Notes

1. Op amps are commercially available in integrated circuit packages in several forms.

可在市场上买到采用多种集成电路封装形式的运算放大器。

2. An input applied to the noninverting terminal will appear with the same polarity at the output, while an input applied to the inverting terminal will appear inverted at the output.

输出与加到同相端的输入极性相同,而与加到反相端的输入极性相反。

3. Although the power supplies are often ignored in op amp circuit diagrams for the sake of simplicity, the power supply currents must not be overlooked.

为了简单起见,在运算放大器的电路图中常省略了电源,但电源的电流一定不能忽略。

4. Thevenin equivalent resistance 戴维南等效电阻

Exercises

I. Translate the phrases into English.

1. 运算放大器　　2. 有源电路　　3. 电子部件　　4. 软件包
5. 管脚　　　　　6. 同相端　　　7. 反相输入　　8. 电路图
9. 压控电压源　　10. 开环增益　　11. 闭环增益　　12. 负反馈
13. 正饱和　　　14. 线性区　　　15. 电压跟随器　16. 等效阻抗

II. Answer the following questions according to the text.

1. How to understand an op amp?
2. Why are op amps popular in practical circuit design?
3. Is the op amp an active element? Why?
4. What is the closed-loop gain?
5. How many modes can the op amp operate in? What are they?
6. How to explain an ideal op amp?
7. What are the characteristics of the ideal op amp?
8. Is a voltage follower a noninverting amplifier or an inverting amplifier?

III. Translate the sentences into Chinese.

1. An op amp is an active circuit element designed to perform mathematical operations of addition, subtraction, multiplication, division, differentiation, and integration.

2. The output section consists of a voltage-controlled source in series with the output resistance R_o.

3. The op amp senses the difference between the two inputs, multiplies it by the gain A, and causes the resulting voltage to appear at the output.

4. An infinite resistance between the input terminals implies that an open circuit exists

there and current cannot enter the op amp.

5. In this circuit, the noninverting input is grounded, u_i is connected to the inverting input through R_1, and the feedback resistor R_f is connected between the inverting input and output.

6. In an inverting amplifier, the output voltage is a negative multiple of the input.

7. The voltage follower minimizes interaction between the two stages and eliminates interstage loading.

Part 6

Digital Logic Circuits

6.1 Basic Concepts

6.1.1 Logic Variables and Digital Words

In digital systems, information is represented by *logic variables* that can assume values of logic 1 or logic 0. The logic value 1 is also called *high*, *true*, or *on*. The logic value 0 is also called *low*, *false*, or *off*. Signals in logic systems switch between high and low as the information being represented changes. We often denote logic variables by uppercase letters such as A, B, and C.

A single binary digit (0 or 1), called a *bit*, represents a very small amount of information. For example, a logic variable R could be used to represent whether or not it is raining in a particular location (say, $R=1$ if it is raining, and $R=0$ if it is not raining).

In order to represent more information, we resort to using groups of logic variables, called *digital words*. For example, the word RWS could be formed in which R represents rain, W is 1 if the wind velocity is greater than 15 miles per hour, and W is 0 if there is less wind. S could be 1 for sunny conditions and 0 for cloudy conditions. Then the digital word 110 would tell us that it is rainy, windy, and cloudy. A *byte* is a word consisting of eight bits, and a *nibble* is a four-bit word.

6.1.2 The AND Gate

One important logic function is called the AND operation. The AND operation on two logic variables, A and B, is represented as AB, read as "A and B". A *truth table* is simply a listing of all of the inputs to a logic operation, together with the corresponding outputs. The truth table for the AND operation of two variables is displayed in Fig. 6.1(a). Notice that AB is 1 only if A and B are both 1. For the AND operation, we can write the following relations:

$$AA = A$$
$$A1 = A$$
$$A0 = 0$$
$$AB = BA$$
$$A(BC) = (AB)C = ABC$$

Circuit symbols for AND gates (i. e., circuits that produce an output equal to the result of the AND operation for all of the inputs) are illustrated in Fig. 6.1(b) and 6.1(c).

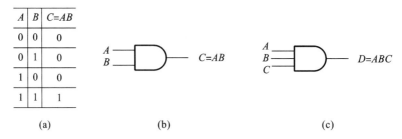

Fig. 6.1 AND operation

(a) Truth table   (b) Symbol for two-input AND gate   (c) Symbol for three-input AND gate

6.1.3 The Logic Inverter

The NOT operation on a logic variable is represented by placing a bar over the symbol for the variable. The symbol $\overline{A}$ is read as "not A" or as "A inverse". If A is 0, $\overline{A}$ is 1. Similarly, if A is 1, $\overline{A}$ is 0.

Circuits that perform the NOT operation are called *inverters*. The truth table and circuit symbol for an inverter are displayed in Fig. 6.2.

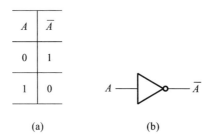

Fig. 6.2 NOT operation

(a) Truth table   (b) Symbol for an inverter

The following results can be established for the NOT operation:

$$A\overline{A} = 0$$
$$\overline{\overline{A}} = A$$

6.1.4 The OR Gate

The OR operation applied to logic variables is written as $A+B$, which is read as "A or B". The truth table for the OR operation and the circuit symbol for the OR gate are shown in Fig. 6.3. Notice that $A+B$ is 1 if A or B (or both) are 1. For the OR operation, we have

$$(A+B)+C = A+(B+C) = A+B+C$$
$$A(B+C) = AB+AC$$

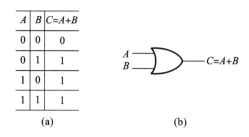

Fig. 6.3 OR operation

(a) Truth table (b) Symbol for two-input OR gate

$$A + 0 = A$$
$$A + 1 = 1$$
$$A + \overline{A} = 1$$
$$A + A = A$$

6.1.5 Boolean Algebra

Although we use the addition sign(+) to represent the OR operation, manipulation of logic variables by the AND, OR, and NOT operations is different from ordinary algebra[1]. The mathematical theory of logic variables and operations is called *Boolean algebra*, named for the mathematician George Boole.

6.1.6 NAND, NOR, and XOR Gates

Some additional logic gates are shown in Fig. 6.4. The NAND gate is equivalent to an AND gate followed by an inverter. Notice that the symbol is the same as that for an AND gate, but with a circle at the output terminal to indicate that the output has been inverted after the AND operation. Similarly, the NOR gate is equivalent to an OR gate followed by an inverter.

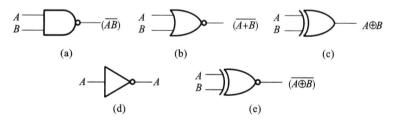

Fig. 6.4 Additional logic-gate symbols

(a) NAND gate (b) NOR gate (c) XOR gate (d) Buffer (e) Equivalence gate

The *exclusive-OR* (XOR) operation for two logic variables A and B is represented by $A \oplus B$ and is defined by

$$0 \oplus 0 = 0$$
$$1 \oplus 0 = 1$$
$$0 \oplus 1 = 1$$
$$1 \oplus 1 = 0$$

Notice that the XOR operation yields 1 if A is 1 or if B is 1, but yields 0 if both A and B are 1. The XOR operation is also known as *modulo-two addition*.

A *buffer* has a single input and produces an output with the same value as the input. (Specially designed buffers are used to provide large currents when a logic signal must be applied to a low-impedance load such as a large capacitance.)

The *equivalent gate* produces a high output only if both inputs have the same value. In effect, it is an XOR followed by an inverter, as the symbol of Fig. 6.4(e) implies.

6.1.7 Logical Sufficiency of NAND Gates and NOR Gates

Two important results in Boolean algebra are De Morgan's laws, which state that

$$AB = \overline{\overline{A} + \overline{B}} \tag{6.1}$$

and

$$A + B = \overline{\overline{AB}} \tag{6.2}$$

Another way to express these laws is as follows: If the variables in a logic expression are replaced by their inverses, and if the AND operation is replaced by OR, the OR operation is replaced by AND, and the expression is inverted, the resulting logic expression yields the same values as before the changes.

If the inputs to a NAND are tied together, an inverter results[2]. This is true because

$$(\overline{AA}) = \overline{A}$$

Also, as shown by Eq. (6.2), the OR operation can be realized by inverting the input variables and combining the results in a NAND gate[3]. This is illustrated in Fig. 6.5, in which the inverters are formed from NAND gates. Finally, a NAND followed by an inverter results in an AND gate. Since the basic logic functions (AND, OR, and NOT) can be realized by using only NAND gates, we conclude that NAND gates are sufficient to realize any combinatorial logic function.

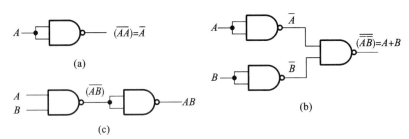

Fig. 6.5 Basic Boolean operations can be implemented with NAND gates. Therefore, any Boolean function can be implemented by the use of NAND gates alone

(a) Inverter   (b) OR gate   (c) AND gate

Similarly, NOR gates are sufficient to realize any combinatorial logic function.

6.2 Electrical Specifications for Logic Gates

In this section, we consider specifications for the actual voltages and currents in logic gates. We reference most of our discussion to the inverter, but the concepts apply to other gates as well.

6.2.1 Logic Ranges

For a given logic family, one range of output voltages represents logic 1, and the other range of voltages represents logic 0. For a particular family of TTL circuits, any output voltage higher than 3.0V represents logic 1, and any voltage lower than 0.5V represents logic 0. Voltages in the transition region between 0.5V and 3V occur only for very short intervals, when the logic value changes. The ranges of voltage assigned to logic 1 and logic 0 are different for each logic family.

For proper operation, a logic circuit only needs to produce a voltage somewhere in the correct range. Thus, component values in digital circuits do not need to be as precise as in analog circuits, for which each amplitude has a different significance.

6.2.2 Positive Versus Negative Logic

Usually, the higher amplitude in a binary system represents 1, and the lower amplitude represents 0. In this case, we say that we have *positive logic*. On the other hand, it is possible to represent 1 by the lower amplitude and 0 by the higher amplitude, resulting in *negative logic*. Unless stated otherwise, we assume positive logic throughout this part.

6.2.3 Input and Output Currents

The reference directions for the input and output currents of an inverter are shown in Fig. 6.6. Note that the reference directions for currents point into the inverter. If the actual currents are in the opposite directions, the values of I_I and I_O are negative. If current flows out of the output terminal (I_O is negative), we say that the inverter *sources* the current. On the other hand, if the current flows into the output terminal, we say that the output *sinks* the current.

The current that the output is capable of sourcing when it is high is denoted by I_{OH}. (I_{OH} has a negative value due to the choice of reference direction.) As the output is called upon to source more current, the output voltage falls because of the output resistance of the gate. The manufacturer guarantees that the gate output voltage will not fall below U_{OH}, as long as the

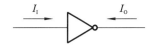

Fig. 6.6 Reference directions for input and output currents (I_O has a negative value if the output sources current)

output source current is smaller in magnitude than I_{OH} and the input signals are in their proper ranges.

Similarly, I_{OL} indicates the maximum current that the output can sink when the gate output is in the low state. In other words, the output voltage is guaranteed to remain below U_{OL}, provided that the gate is not required to sink a current greater than I_{OL} and that the input signals are in their proper ranges.

The worst-case (maximum magnitude) input current, provided that the input voltage is in the acceptable logic-0 input range, is denoted by I_{IL}. Similarly, the worst-case input current for a high input is denoted by I_{IH}. For some types of logic circuits, current flows out of the input terminal when logic 0 is applied. Current usually flows into the input terminal for a logic-1 input.

New Words and Expressions

1. uppercase letter　大写字母
2. binary digit　二进制位，二进制数字
3. resort to　依靠，采取
4. nibble　*n.* 半字节
5. together with　和，连同
6. inverter　*n.* 反相器
7. Boolean algebra　布尔代数
8. manipulation　*n.* 操作，处理
9. buffer　*n.* 缓冲器
10. exclusive　*adj.* 独有的，排外的
11. exclusive-OR　"异"或
12. modulo　*prep.* 以……为模
13. equivalent gate　等效门
14. sufficiency　*n.* 足够，充足
15. logic expression　逻辑表达式
16. tie　*v.* 连接，系
17. combinatorial　*adj.* 组合的
18. electrical specification　电气特性
19. logic family　逻辑系列
20. source　*v.* 找出……的来源
21. sink　*v.* 下沉，渗透
22. call upon　要求
23. guarantee　*v.* 保证

Notes

1. Although we use the addition sign (+) to represent the OR operation, manipulation of logic variables by the AND, OR, and NOT operations is different from ordinary algebra.

尽管用加号来表示"或"运算，但是逻辑变量的"与""或""非"运算与普通的代数运算是不同的。

2. If the inputs to a NAND are tied together, an inverter results.

如果将与非门的两个输入端连到一起，与非门就变成了反相器。

3. The OR operation can be realized by inverting the input variables and combining the

results in a NAND gate.

将输入变量取反后再与非门组合在一起就能实现"或"运算。

Exercises

I. Translate the phrases into English.

1. 逻辑变量 2. 位 3. 数字字 4. 字节 5. 半字节
6. 与运算 7. 真值表 8. 与门 9. 非门 10. 或门
11. 加号 12. 与非门 13. 异或运算 14. 逻辑表达式 15. 二进制
16. 正逻辑 17. 负逻辑 18. 参考方向

II. Answer the following questions according to the text.

1. What is a byte? What is a nibble?
2. What is an inverter?
3. What is the mathematical theory of logic variables and operations called?
4. Which gate is an AND gate followed by an inverter equivalent to?
5. What is the effect of buffers?

III. Translate the sentences into Chinese.

1. A truth table is simply a listing of all of the inputs to a logic operation, together with the corresponding outputs.

2. The NOT operation on a logic variable is represented by placing a bar over the symbol for the variable.

3. A buffer has a single input and produces an output with the same value as the input.

4. The equivalent gate produces a high output only if both inputs have the same value. In effect, it is an XOR followed by an inverter.

5. If the variables in a logic expression are replaced by their inverses, and if the AND operation is replaced by OR, the OR operation is replaced by AND, and the expression is inverted, the resulting logic expression yields the same values as before the changes.

6. If current flows out of the output terminal (I_O is negative), we say that the inverter sources the current. On the other hand, if the current flows into the output terminal, we say that the output sinks the current.

Part 7

Transformers

7.1 Introduction

In general, a transformer is a *static* electromagnetic machine (i. e., it has no moving parts). Transformers are commonly used for changing the voltage and current levels in a given electrical system, establishing electrical isolation, impedance matching, and measuring instruments. Power and distribution transformers are used extensively in electrical power systems to generate the electrical power at the most economical generator voltage level; to transmit and distribute electrical power at the most economical voltage level; and to utilize power at the most economical, suitable, and safe voltage level.

Isolating transformers are used to electrically isolate electric circuits from each other or to block DC signals while maintaining AC continuity between the circuits, and to eliminate electromagnetic noise in many types of circuits. Transformers are widely used in communication systems that vary in frequency from audio to radio to video levels. They perform various tasks, such as impedance matching for improved power transfer, and are used as input transformers, output transformers, and insulation apparatus between electric circuits, and interstage transformers. Transformers are used in the whole frequency spectrum in electrical circuits, from near DC to hundreds of megahertz, including both continuous sinusoidal and phase waveforms. For example, they can be found in use at power line frequencies (between 60 and 400Hz), audio frequencies (20 to 20000Hz), ultrasonic frequencies (20000 to 100000Hz), and radio frequencies (over 300kHz).

Transformers are also used in measuring instruments. Instrument transformers are used to measure high voltages and large currents with standard small-range voltmeters (120V), ammeters (5A), and wattmeters, and to transform voltages and currents to activate relays for control and protection. *Voltage transformers* (VTs) (also known as PTs, i. e., *potential transformers*) are single-phase transformers that are used to step down the voltage to be measured to a safe value. *Current transformers* (CTs) are used to step down currents to measurable levels. The secondaries of both voltage and current transformers are normally grounded.

A transformer consists of a primary winding and a secondary winding linked by a mutual magnetic field. Transformers may have an air core, an iron core, or a variable core, depending upon their operating frequency and application. Transformers are also quite different in size and shape depending on the application. In power systems applications, the single- or three-phase transformers with ratings up to 500kVA are defined as *distribution transformers*, whereas those transformers with ratings over 500kVA at voltage levels of 69 kV and above, are defined as *power transformers*.

A transformer is basically made up of two or more windings coupled by a mutual magnetic field. Ferromagnetic cores are employed to develop tight magnetic coupling and high flux densities. When such a coupling exists, the transformer is called an *iron-core transformer*. Most distribution and power transformers are immersed in a tank of oil for better insulation and cooling purposes. The leads of the windings are brought to the outside of the tank through insulating bushings which are attached to the tank. Such transformers are used in high-power applications. When there is no ferromagnetic material but only air present, such a transformer is called an *air-core transformer*. These transformers have poor magnetic coupling and are usually used in lower-power applications such as in electronic circuits. In this part the focus is set exclusively on *iron-core transformers*.

7.2 Transformer Construction

The magnetic cores of transformers used in power systems are built either in core type or shell type, as shown in Fg. 7.1. In either case, the magnetic cores are made up of stacks of laminations cut from silicon-steel sheets[1]. Silicon-steel sheets usually contain about 3 percent silicon and 97 percent steel. The silicon content decreases the magnetizing losses, especially the ones due to hysteresis loss. The laminations are coated with a nonconducting and insulating varnish on one side. Such a laminated core substantially reduces the core loss due to eddy currents. Most laminated materials are cold rolled and often specially annealed to orient the grain or iron crystals[2]. This causes a very high permeability and low hysteresis to flux in the direction of rolling. Thus, in turn, it requires a lower exciting current. The laminations for the core-type transformer, shown in Fig. 7.1(a), may be made up of L-shape, or U-and I-shaped laminations. The core for the shell-type transformer, shown in Fig. 7.1(b), is usually made up of E- and I-shaped laminations. To minimize the use of copper and decrease copper loss, the magnetic cores of large transformers are built in stepped cores, as shown in Fig. 7.2.

Figure 7.1(a) shows a *core-type construction* that has the total number of primary winding turns located on one leg of the core and the total number of secondary winding turns placed on the other leg. This design causes large leakage flux and therefore results in a smaller mutual flux for a given primary voltage. To keep the leakage flux within a few percent of the mutual flux, each winding may be divided into two coils; the two half coils

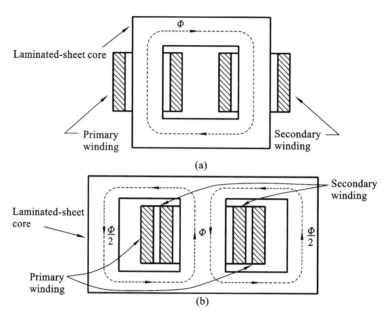

Fig. 7.1　Transformer core construction
(a) Core type　(b) Shell type

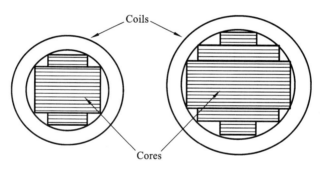

Fig. 7.2　Stepped transformer cores

are then mounted on two sides of the rectangle. A large reduction in leakage flux can be obtained by further subdividing and sandwiching the primary and secondary turns, however, at considerable cost[3]. Leakage flux can be greatly decreased by using the *shell-type construction* shown in Fig. 7.1(b). However, the steel-to-copper weight ratio is greater in the shell-type transformer. It is more efficient but more costly in material. The coils employed in shell-type transformers are usually of a "*pancake*" form unlike the cylindrical forms used in the core-type transformer, where the coils are placed one on top of the other, the low-voltage winding is placed closer to the core with the high-voltage winding on top[4]. This design simplifies the problem of insulating the high-voltage winding from the core and reduces the leakage flux considerably.

7.3 The Ideal Transformer

Consider a transformer with two windings, a primary winding of N_1 turns and a secondary winding of N_2 turns, as shown in Fig. 7.3(a). The core is made up of a ferromagnetic material. Assume that the transformer is an *ideal transformer* with the following properties:

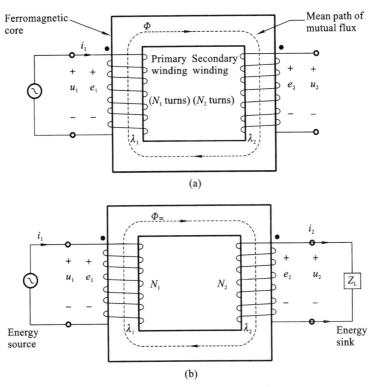

Fig. 7.3 Ideal transformer
(a) With no load (b) With load

- The winding resistances are negligible.
- All magnetic flux is confined to the ferromagnetic core and links both windings, i.e., leakage fluxes do not exist.
- The core losses are negligible.
- The permeability of the core material is almost infinite so that negligible net magnetic motive force (mmf) is required to establish the flux in the core. In other words, the excitation current required to establish flux in the core is negligible.
- The magnetic core material does not saturate.

If the primary winding is connected to an energy source with a time-varying voltage u_1, a time-varying flux Φ and a flux linkage λ_1 of winding N_1 is established in the core. If

u_1 varies over time, then i_1, Φ and λ_1 will vary over time, and an electromotive force (emf) e_2 will be induced in winding N_1. Therefore,

$$u_1 = e_1 = \frac{d\lambda_1}{dt} = N_1 \frac{d\Phi}{dt} \tag{7.1}$$

Because there is no leakage flux, the flux Φ must link all N_2 turns of the secondary winding. Since the resistance of the secondary winding is assumed to be zero in an ideal transformer, it induces a voltage e_2 which is the same as the terminal voltage u_2. Thus,

$$u_2 = e_2 = \frac{d\lambda_2}{dt} = N_2 \frac{d\Phi}{dt} \tag{7.2}$$

From Eqs. (7.1) and (7.2),

$$\frac{u_1}{u_2} = \frac{e_1}{e_2} = \frac{N_1}{N_2} = \alpha \tag{7.3}$$

which may also be written in terms of root mean square (rms) values as

$$\frac{U_1}{U_2} = \frac{E_1}{E_2} = \frac{N_1}{N_2} = \alpha \tag{7.4}$$

where α is known as the *turns ratio*. Note that the potential ratio is equal to the turns ratio. (Here, lowercase letters are used for instantaneous values and uppercase letters are used for rms values.) From Eq. (7.4),

$$U_1 = \frac{N_1}{N_2} U_2 = \alpha U_2 \tag{7.5}$$

Assume that a load (energy sink) with an impedance Z_L is connected at the terminals of the secondary winding, as shown in 7.3(b). Therefore, a load current (i.e., secondary current) will flow in the secondary winding. Since the core of an ideal transformer is infinitely permeable, the net mmf will always be zero. Thus,

$$N_1 i_1 - N_2 i_2 = \Phi R = 0 \tag{7.6}$$

where R is the reluctance of the magnetic core. Since the reluctance of a magnetic core of a well-designed modern transformer is very small (almost zero) before the core is saturated, then

$$N_1 i_1 - N_2 i_2 = 0 \tag{7.7}$$

or

$$N_1 i_1 = N_2 i_2 \tag{7.8}$$

That is, the primary and secondary mmfs are equal and opposite in direction. From Eq. (7.8),

$$\frac{i_1}{i_2} = \frac{N_2}{N_1} = \frac{1}{\alpha} \tag{7.9}$$

which may be written in terms of rms values as

$$\frac{I_1}{I_2} = \frac{N_2}{N_1} = \frac{1}{\alpha} \tag{7.10}$$

Hence, the currents in the windings are inversely proportional to the turns of the windings. From Eq. (7.10),

$$I_1 = \frac{N_2}{N_1}I_2 = \frac{I_2}{\alpha} \tag{7.11}$$

From Eqs. (7.3) and (7.9),

$$u_1 i_1 = u_2 i_2 \tag{7.12}$$

or in terms of rms values

$$U_1 I_1 = \left(\frac{N_1}{N_2}U_2\right)\left(\frac{N_2}{N_1}I_2\right) = U_2 I_2 \tag{7.13}$$

That is, in an ideal transformer, the input power (VA) is equal to the output power (VA). In other words, the value of the apparent power remains the same. This is the *power invariance principle* which means that the volt-amperes are conserved. Furthermore, the complex power supplied to the primary is equal to the complex power delivered by the secondary to the load. Thus,

$$\boldsymbol{U}_1 \boldsymbol{I}_1^* = \boldsymbol{U}_2 \boldsymbol{I}_2^* \tag{7.14}$$

In the event that the primary and secondary turns are equal, these transformers are usually known as the *isolating transformers*, as previously stated. In power systems, if the number of turns of the secondary winding is greater than the number of turns of the primary winding, the transformer is known as a *step-up transformer*. On the other hand, if the number of turns of the primary winding is greater than that of the secondary winding, the transformer is known as a *step-down transformer*.

New Words and Expressions

1. transformer   *n.* 变压器
2. static   *adj.* 静态的,静电的
3. electromagnetic   *adj.* 电磁的
4. isolation   *n.* 绝缘
5. extensively   *adv.* 广阔地,广大地
6. block   *v.* 阻止,阻塞
7. continuity   *n.* 连续性,持续性
8. spectrum   *n.* 频谱,光谱
9. megahertz   *n.* 兆赫
10. power line   电力线,输电线
11. ultrasonic   *adj.* 超声的
12. instrument   *n.* 仪器,工具
13. secondary   *adj.* 次要的,第二的
14. mutual   *adj.* 共同的,相互的
15. rating   *n.* 等级,额定功率
16. ferromagnetic   *adj.* 铁磁的
17. flux   *n.* 流量
18. density   *n.* 密度
19. immerse   *v.* 沉浸
20. bushing   *n.* 套管,轴衬
21. exclusively   *adv.* 唯一地,专有地
22. stack   *n.* 堆,堆叠,堆栈
23. lamination   *n.* 薄板,迭片结构
24. magnetizing   *n.* 磁化
25. hysteresis   *n.* 磁滞现象
26. varnish   *n.* 清漆,亮光漆
27. eddy   *n.* 涡流,漩涡
28. roll   *v.* 压平,辗
29. anneal   *v.* 使退火,使坚韧
30. grain   *n.* 颗粒,纹理

31. crystal   *n.* 晶体,结晶
32. permeability   *n.* 渗透性,渗磁率
33. step   *v.* 迈步   *n.* 梯阶
34. mutual flux   互(感)磁通
35. rectangle   *n.* 矩形,长方形
36. subdivide   *v.* 把……细分
37. sandwich   *v.* 夹入……中间
38. pancake   *n.* 薄烤饼
39. confine   *v.* 限制
40. magnetic motive force   磁动势
41. flux linkage   磁链
42. reluctance   *n.* 磁阻
43. invariance   *n.* 不变性,恒定性

Notes

1. In either case, the magnetic cores are made up of stacks of laminations cut from silicon-steel sheets.

无论哪种铁芯都是由从硅钢片上剪下的铁芯叠片叠装而成的。

2. Most laminated materials are cold rolled and often specially annealed to orient the grain or iron crystals.

大多数叠片为冷轧的,且常常经过特殊的退火处理用以定位铁芯中的颗粒或晶体。

3. A large reduction in leakage flux can be obtained by further subdividing and sandwiching the primary and secondary turns, however, at considerable cost.

进一步细分绕组并增加原边和副边的匝数可大大降低漏磁通,但成本却提高许多。

4. The coils employed in shell-type transformers are usually of a "*pancake*" form unlike the cylindrical forms used in the core-type transformer, where the coils are placed one on top of the other, the low-voltage winding is placed closer to the core with the high-voltage winding on top.

芯式变压器的线圈采用圆柱结构,与之不同,壳式变压器的线圈通常采用饼形结构。芯式变压器中一个线圈位于另一个之上,并且高压线圈在上,低压线圈更靠近铁芯。

Exercises

I. Translate the phrases into English.

1. 理想变压器   2. 电气绝缘   3. 阻抗匹配   4. 电力
5. 绝缘变压器   6. 电压互感器   7. 电流互感器   8. 原边绕组
9. 工作频率   10. 配电变压器   11. 电力变压器   12. 磁通密度
13. 磁场   14. 铁芯变压器   15. 大功率   16. 空芯
17. 磁耦合   18. 小功率   19. 励磁损耗   20. 磁滞损耗
21. 涡流   22. 励磁电流   23. 漏磁通   24. 互磁通
25. 线圈   26. 芯式   27. 壳式   28. 高压绕组

29. 磁链   30. 电动势   31. 有效值   32. 匝数比
33. 视在功率   34. 匝数   35. 升压变压器   36. 降压变压器

II. Answer the following questions according to the text.

1. Why is a transformer a static electromagnetic machine?
2. What is the effect of isolating transformers?
3. What are the transformers with ratings up to 500kVA defined as? What are the transformers with ratings over 500kVA and at voltage levels of 69kV and above called?
4. What is the turns ratio?
5. What is the relationship between the turns ratio and the potential ratio of the ideal transformer?
6. What is the relationship between the primary turns and secondary turns of the isolating transformer? How is the step-up transformer? How is the step-down transformer?

III. Translate the sentences into Chinese.

1. Transformers are commonly used for changing the voltage and current levels in a given electrical system, establishing electrical isolation, impedance matching, and measuring instruments.
2. Voltage transformers are single-phase transformers that are used to step down the voltage to be measured to a safe value. Current transformers are used to step down currents to measurable levels.
3. Lowercase letters are used for instantaneous values and uppercase letters are used for rms values.
4. The reluctance of a magnetic core of a well-designed modern transformer is very small (almost zero) before the core is saturated.
5. The currents in the windings are inversely proportional to the turns of the windings.

Part 8

Electrical Machines

8.1 A Brief Overview

In general, an electrical machine can be defined as an apparatus that can be used either to convert electrical energy into mechanical energy or to convert mechanical energy into electrical energy. If such a machine is used to convert electrical energy into mechanical energy, it is called *a motor*; however, if it is used to convert mechanical energy into electrical energy, it is called a *generator*. Any given machine can convert energy in either direction and can therefore be used either as a motor or as a generator. Such conversion is facilitated through the action of a magnetic field[1]. A generator has a rotary motion provided by a prime mover which supplies mechanical energy input. The relative motion between the conductors and the magnetic field of a generator produces an electrical energy output. On the other hand, a motor has electrical energy supplied to its windings and a magnetic field that generates an electromagnetic interaction to produce mechanical energy or torque.

In general, each machine has a nonmoving (i.e., stationary) part and a moving (i.e., nonstationary) part. Depending on whether such a machine functions as a generator or motor, the moving part that is attached to a mechanical system receives mechanical input or provides mechanical output. The motion of such a moving part can be linear (e.g., as in *linear motors*); vibrating or reciprocating (e.g., as in various electrical razors); or rotating.

In this part, only the rotating electrical machines will be reviewed. They include ①polyphase synchronous machines, ② polyphase induction (also called *asynchronous*) machines, and ③DC machines. However, there are other rotating and linear machines that will not be included here. They operate basically on the same principles.

Rotating electrical machines have an outside (i.e., *stationary*) part which is called the stator and an inner (i.e., *rotating*) part which is called the rotor. As shown in Fig. 8.1, the rotor is centered within the stator, and the space that is located between the outside of the rotor and the inside of the stator is called the air gap. The figure shows that the rotor is supported by a steel rod which is called a shaft. In turn, the shaft is supported by bearings so that the rotor can turn freely. Both the rotor and stator of a rotating machine, as well as

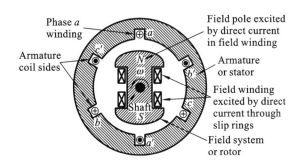

Fig. 8.1 Basic structure of an elementary three-phase two-pole AC generator

a transformer, have windings.

8.2 Induction Machines

8.2.1 Introduction

Because of its relatively low cost, simple and rugged construction, minimal maintenance requirements, and good operating characteristics which satisfy a wide variety of loads, the induction motor is the most commonly used type of AC motor. Induction motors range in size from a few watts to about 40000hp(1 hp = 746 W). Small fractional-horsepower motors are usually single-phase and are used extensively for domestic appliances such as refrigerators, washers, dryers, and blenders. Large induction motors (usually above 5 horsepower) are always designed for three-phase operation to achieve a constant torque and balanced network loading. In particular, where very large machinery is to be operated, the three-phase induction motor is the *workhorse* of the industry. In contrast to DC motors, induction motors can operate from supplies in excess of 10kV.

In typical induction motors, the stator winding (the *field winding*) is connected to the source, and the rotor winding (the *armature winding*) is short-circuited for many applications, or may be closed through external resistances. Thus, an induction motor is a *singly excited* motor (as opposed to a *doubly excited* synchronous motor). In such a motor, alternating current passing through a fixed stator winding sets up a rotating magnetic field. This moving field induces the current in closed loops of wire mounted on the rotor. These currents set up magnetic fields around the wires and cause them to follow the main magnetic field as it rotates. Therefore, the operation of the induction motor depends on the rotating field passing through the loops on the rotor, which must always turn more slowly than the rotating field. Since no current has to be supplied to the rotor, the induction motor is simple to construct and reliable in operation. This class of rotating machines derives its name from the fact that the rotor current results from *induction*, rather than *conduction*. A given induction machine can be operated in the motor region, generator region, or braking region, as shown in Fig. 8.2. In the *motor mode*, its operating speed is slightly lower than its synchronous speed; but, in the *generator mode*, its operating speed is slightly higher than its synchronous speed and it needs magnetizing reactive power from the system that it is connected to in order to supply power. The full-load speed of three-phase induction motors is often within 7 percent of the synchronous speed, even though full-load speeds of 1 percent below the synchronous speed are not uncommon.

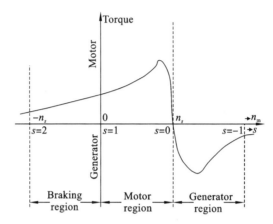

Fig. 8.2 An induction machine's torque-speed characteristic curve showing braking, motor, and generator regions

In the *braking mode* of operation, a three-phase induction motor running at a steady-state speed can be brought to a quick stop by interchanging two of its stator leads[2]. By doing this, the phase sequence, and therefore the direction of rotation of the magnetic field, is suddenly reversed; the motor comes to a stop under the influence of torque and is immediately disconnected from the line before it can start in the other direction. This is also known as the *plugging operation*.

Since the induction motor cannot produce its excitation, it needs reactive power; it draws a lagging current from the source and operates at a power factor that is less than unity (usually, above 0.85). However, it runs at lower lagging power factors when lightly loaded. To limit the reactive power, the magnetizing reactance has to be high, and thus the air gap is shorter than in synchronous motors of the same size and rating (with the exception of small motors). Also, the starting current of an induction motor is usually five to seven times its full-load (i. e., rated) current. In general, the speed of an induction motor is not easily controlled.

Even though the induction machine, with a wound rotor, can be used as a generator, its performance characteristics (especially in comparison to a synchronous generator) have not been found satisfactory for most applications. However, induction generators are occasionally used at hydroelectric power plants. Also, the induction machine with a wound rotor can be used as a *frequency changer*.

8.2.2 Induced Voltages

Assume that the rotor winding is wound-type, wye-connected and open-circuited. Since the rotor winding is open-circuited, no torque can develop. This represents the *standstill operation* of a three-phase induction motor. The application of a three-phase voltage to the three-phase stator winding results in a rotating magnetic field that "cuts" both the stator and rotor windings at the supply frequency f_1. Hence, the rms value of the induced voltage per phase of the rotor winding can be expressed as

$$E_2 = \frac{2\pi}{\sqrt{2}} f_1 N_2 \phi k_{w2} \tag{8.1}$$

or

$$E_2 = 4.44 f_1 N_2 \phi k_{w2} \tag{8.2}$$

where the subscripts 1 and 2 are used to denote stator- and rotor-winding quantities, respectively. Since the rotor is at standstill, the stator frequency f_1 is used in Eqs. (8.1) and (8.2). Here, the flux ϕ is the mutual flux per pole involving both the stator and rotor windings. Similarly, the rms value of the induced voltage per phase of the stator winding can be expressed as

$$E_1 = 4.44 f_1 N_1 \phi k_{w1} \tag{8.3}$$

where k_{w1} and k_{w2} are the winding factors for the stator and rotor windings, respectively.

8.3 Synchronous Machines

8.3.1 Introduction

Almost all three-phase power is generated by three-phase synchronous machines operated as generators. Synchronous generators are also called *alternators* and are normally large machines producing electrical power at hydro, nuclear, or thermal power plants. Efficiency and economy-of-scale dictate the use of very large generators. Because of this, synchronous generators rated in excess of 1000MVA (mega-volt-amperes) are quite commonly used in generating stations. Large synchronous generators have a high efficiency which at ratings greater than 50MVA usually exceeds 98 percent. The term *synchronous* refers to the fact that these machines operate at constant speeds and frequencies under steady-state operations.

A given synchronous machine can operate as a generator or as a motor. Such machines are used as motors in constant-speed drives in industrial applications and also for pumped-storage stations. In small sizes with only fractional horsepower, they are used in electric clocks, timers, record players, and in other applications which require constant speed. Synchronous motors with frequency changers such as inverters or cycloconverters can also be used in variable-speed drive applications. An overexcited synchronous motor with no load can be used as a *synchronous capacitor* or *synchronous condenser* to correct power factors.

8.3.2 Construction of Synchronous Machines

In a synchronous machine, the *armature* winding is on the stator and the *field* winding is on the rotor. In normal operation the three-phase stator currents (in the three-phase distributed stator winding) set up a rotating magnetic field. The synchronous machine *rotors* are simply rotating electromagnets which have the same number of poles as the stator winding. The rotor winding is supplied from an external DC source through slip rings and brushes; therefore, it produces a rotor magnetic field. Since the rotor rotates in synchronism with the stator magnetic field, the total magnetic field is the result of these two fields.

A synchronous machine is a constant-speed (i.e., synchronous speed) machine. Its rotor structure therefore depends on its speed rating. For this reason, high-speed machines have cylindrical (or non-salient pole) rotors, whereas low-speed machines have salient pole rotors. With a cylindrical rotor the reluctance of the magnetic circuit of the field is independent of its actual direction and relative to the direct axis[3]. However, with salient poles the reluctance is lowest when the field is along the direct axis where the air-gap is the minimum. It is highest when the field is directly halfway between the poles, that is, along the quadrature axis[4].

The stator of a synchronous machine is basically similar to that of a three-phase induction machine. The stator winding is the source of voltage and electric power when the machine is operating as a generator, and the input winding when it is operating as a motor. It is usually made of preformed stator coils in a double-layer winding. The winding itself is distributed and chorded to reduce the harmonic content of the output voltages and currents.

8.4 Direct-Current Machines

8.4.1 Introduction

A direct-current (DC) machine is a versatile machine, that is, the same machine can be used as a generator to convert mechanical energy to DC electrical energy or as a motor to convert DC electrical energy into mechanical energy. However, the use of DC machines as DC generators to produce bulk power has rapidly disappeared due to the economic advantages involved in the use of alternating-current generation, transmission, and distribution. This is partly due to the high efficiency and relative simplicity with which transformers convert voltages from one level to another. Today, the need for DC power is often met by the use of solid-state-controlled rectifiers. However, DC motors are used extensively in many industrial applications because they provide constant mechanical power output or constant torque, adjustable motor speed over wide ranges, precise speed or position control, efficient operation over a wide speed range, rapid acceleration and deceleration, and responsiveness to feedback signals. Such machines can vary in size from miniature permanent-magnet motors to machines rated for continuous operation at several thousand horsepower. Examples of small DC motors include those used for small control devices, wind-shield-wiper motors, fan motors, starter motors, and various servomotors[5]. Application examples for larger DC motors include industrial drive motors in conveyors, pumps, hoists, overhead cranes, forklifts, fans, steel and aluminum rolling mills, paper mills, textile mills, various other rolling mills, golf carts, electrical cars, street cars or trolleys, electric trains, electric elevators, and large earth-moving equipment[6]. Obviously, DC machine applications are very significant, but the advantages of the DC machine must be weighed against its greater initial investment cost and the maintenance problems associated with its brush-commutator system[7].

8.4.2 Armature Voltage

In a DC machine the armature voltage is the internal generated voltage. It can be expressed as

$$E_a = K_{a1} \Phi_d n_m \tag{8.4}$$

where

$$K_{a1} = \frac{Zp}{60\alpha} \tag{8.5}$$

Therefore, the armature voltage is a function of the flux in the machine, the speed of its rotor, and a constant that depends on the machine.

The armature voltage, or more precisely the internal generated voltage, is not the terminal voltage. Consider the circuit representation of a separately excited DC generator and motor as shown in Fig. 8.3(a) and Fig. 8.3(b), respectively. The armature voltage E_a can be expressed as

$$E_a = U_t \pm I_a R_a \tag{8.6}$$

where the plus sign is used for a generator and the minus sign for a motor. U_t is the terminal voltage and R_a is the armature resistance. Therefore, in the case of a generator, the armature voltage is always greater than the terminal voltage. In a motor, the armature voltage is less than the terminal voltage.

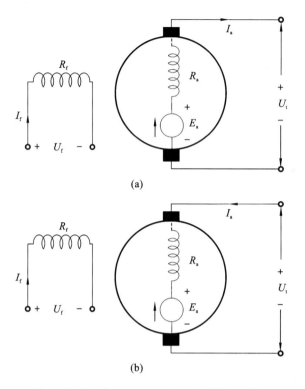

Fig. 8.3 Simple representation of a DC machine
(a) Circuit representation of a DC generator (b) Circuit representation of a DC motor

New Words and Expressions

1. facilitate   *v.* 促进,使容易
2. rotary   *adj.* 旋转的
3. prime mover   原动力
4. stationary   *adj.* 静止的
5. be attached to   附属于
6. linear   *adj.* 直线的
7. reciprocate   *v.* 往复运动
8. razor   *n.* 剃须刀,剃刀
9. rotate   *v.* 旋转
10. polyphase   *adj.* 多相的
11. synchronous   *adj.* 同步的
12. induction   *n.* 感应
13. asynchronous   *adj.* 异步的
14. center   *v.* 集中,居中
15. armature   *n.* 电枢
16. field winding   励磁绕组
17. slip ring   滑环
18. elementary   *adj.* 基本的
19. rod   *n.* 棒,杆
20. bearing   *n.* 轴承
21. rugged   *adj.* 坚固的
22. fractional horsepower   小功率
23. domestic   *adj.* 家庭的,国内的
24. blender   *n.* 搅拌机
25. workhorse   *n.* 重负荷机器
26. lead   *n.* 导线
27. plugging   *n.* 反向制动,堵塞
28. lagging   *adj.* 滞后的,落后的

29. reactance   *n.* 电抗
30. wound rotor   绕线转子
31. hydroelectric   *adj.* 水力发电的
32. frequency changer   变频器
33. standstill   *n.* 停止,静止
34. subscript   *n.* 下标
35. pumped-storage   抽水蓄能
36. electric clock   电钟,电计时器
37. inverter   *n.* 逆变器,换流器
38. cycloconverter   *n.* 周波变换器
39. condenser   *n.* 电容器,冷凝器
40. salient   *adj.* 突出的
41. direct axis   直轴
42. quadrature axis   交轴,正交轴
43. chord   *v.* 调和   *n.* 弦
44. versatile   *adj.* 通用的
45. bulk   *n.* 大块,大多数
46. acceleration   *n.* 加速
47. miniature   *adj.* 小规模的,微型的
48. permanent   *adj.* 永久的,永恒的

Notes

1. Such conversion is facilitated through the action of a magnetic field.
be facilitated   变得更为方便
在磁场的作用下这样的转换变得更为方便。

2. In the braking mode of operation, a three-phase induction motor running at a steady-state speed can be brought to a quick stop by interchanging two of its stator leads.
运行在稳态转速的三相感应电机通过互换两根定子接线就可以运行在制动状态并快速停下来。

3. With a cylindrical rotor the reluctance of the magnetic circuit of the field is independent of its actual direction and relative to the direct axis.
圆柱形转子其磁场磁路的磁阻与直轴有关,与磁场的实际方向无关。

4. It is highest when the field is directly halfway between the poles, that is, along the quadrature axis.
当磁场正好处于磁极的中间时,也就是沿着交轴方向时,磁阻最大。

5. Examples of small DC motors include those used for small control devices, wind-shield-wiper motors, fan motors, starter motors, and various servomotors.
wind-shield-wiper 风挡刮水; fan 风扇; servomotor 伺服电机
小型直流电机的例子包括小型控制装置中所用的电机、风挡刮水电机、风扇电机、启动器电机及各种伺服电机。

6. Application examples for larger DC motors include industrial drive motors in conveyors, pumps, hoists, overhead cranes, forklifts, fans, steel and aluminum rolling mills, paper mills, textile mills, various other rolling mills, golf carts, electrical cars, street cars or trolleys, electric trains, electric elevators, and large earth-moving equipment.
conveyor 传送带; hoist 起重机; overhead crane 高架起重机; forklift 铲车;

fan 鼓风机；rolling mill 轧钢机；textile mill 纺织机；golf cart 高尔夫球手推车； street car 电车；electric elevator 电梯；earth-moving equipment 运土设备

传送带、泵、起重机、高架起重机、铲车、风机、钢和铝轧机、造纸机、纺织机、其他各种轧钢机、高尔夫球手推车、电动车、电气火车、电梯以及大型运土设备中所用的驱动电机都是较大直流电机应用实例。

7. Obviously, DC machine applications are very significant, but the advantages of the DC machine must be weighed against its greater initial investment cost and the maintenance problems associated with its brush-commutator system.

weighed against 权衡，与……比较，对……不利

显然，直流电机的应用非常有意义，但是也存在初期成本投入较高、电刷-换向器系统维修困难等问题，应用时一定要权衡其利弊。

Exercises

I. Translate the phrases into English.

1. 电动机　　2. 发电机　　3. 机械能　　4. 电能　　5. 电磁的
6. 直线式电动机　7. 同步电机　8. 感应电机　9. 定子　　10. 转子
11. 气隙　　12. 轴　　13. 电枢　　14. 励磁绕组　15. 无功功率
16. 制动状态　17. 稳态　　18. 相序　　19. 反向制动的　20. 滞后电流
21. 励磁电抗　22. 启动电流　23. 变频器　24. 感应电势　25. 逆变器
26. 周波变换器　27. 换向器

II. Answer the following questions according to the text.

1. What is a motor? What is a generator?
2. Why is the induction motor widely used?
3. What is the relationship between the rotating field passing through the loops in the rotor and the rotating field of the induction motor?
4. Why is the induction motor simple to construct and reliable in operation?
5. How many regions can an induction machine be operated in? What are they?
6. What are most of the three-phase power generated by?
7. What advantages do DC motors have?
8. What does the armature voltage depend on in a DC motor?

III. Translate the sentences into Chinese.

1. Depending on whether such a machine functions as a generator or motor, the moving part that is attached to a mechanical system receives mechanical input or provides mechanical output.

2. The rotor is centered within the stator, and the space that is located between the outside of the rotor and the inside of the stator is called the air gap.

3. In the motor mode, its operating speed is slightly less than its synchronous speed;

but, in the generator mode, its operating speed is slightly greater than its synchronous speed and it needs magnetizing reactive power from the system that it is connected to in order to supply power.

4. Since the induction motor cannot produce its excitation, it needs reactive power; it draws a lagging current from the source and operates at a power factor that is less than unity (usually, above 0.85).

5. The application of a three-phase voltage to the three-phase stator winding results in a rotating magnetic field that "cuts" both the stator and rotor windings at the supply frequency f_1.

6. The rotor winding is supplied from an external DC source through slip rings and brushes; therefore, it produces a rotor magnetic field.

7. The term synchronous refers to the fact that these machines operate at constant speeds and frequencies under steady-state operations.

8. The plus sign is used for a generator and the minus sign for a motor. In the case of a generator, the armature voltage is always greater than the terminal voltage. In a motor, the armature voltage is less than the terminal voltage.

科技英语学习要点(一)——科技英语的特点

随着现代科学技术的发展,科技英语(English for Science and Technology,简称 EST)已发展成为一种重要的英语文体,它与新闻报刊文体、论述文体、公文文体、描述及叙述文体、应用文体共同构成英语六大主要文体。自 20 世纪 70 年代以来,国际上对科技英语给予了极大关注,有不少学者对其进行了专门研究。

从广义上说,所谓科技英语,泛指一切论及或谈及科学或技术的书面语和口头语。具体说,其包括以下几个方面:

① 科技著述、科技论文(或科技报告)、实验报告(或实验方案)等;
② 各类科技情报及其他文字资料;
③ 科技实用手册,包括仪器、仪表、机械和工具等的结构描述文字资料和操作规程的叙述资料;
④ 有关科技问题的会议、会谈及交谈用语;
⑤ 科技影片或录像等有声资料的解说词等。

1.1 Characteristics of Vocabulary
（词汇的特点）

- 大量使用专业词汇

(1) 常用词汇专业化

例如:

current	流通→电流	loop	圈→(电路)回路
flux	通量→磁通	brush	刷子→电刷
piece	片→零部件	mouth	口→开度
gain	盈利→增益	desk	书桌→控制屏

(2) 同一词语词义专业化

例如:

transmission	电气工程专业:输送
	无线电专业:发射、播送
	机械学:传动、变速
	物理学:透射
	医学:遗传
power	数学:幂、乘方

	物理学:功率
	光学:放大率、焦强
	机械学:动力
	统计学:功放
	电气工程:电力、动力
phase	土壤学:分段
	物理学:相
	电工学:相位
	数学:位相
	动物学:型
	天文学:周相
resistance	力学:阻力
	电学:电阻
	机械学:耐受性、强度

(3) 广泛运用构词法,形成丰富多彩的专业词汇

英语专业词汇除采用常用词汇专业化和同一词语词义专业化的方法外,还采用英语其他构词法,大量构筑新的专业词汇,以扩充专业词汇量。其数量之多、变化速度之快,远非英语中的其他文体所能及。

例如:

pulse-scaler	脉冲定标器
electromechanical＝electric＋mechanical	机电的
electrochemical＝electric＋chemical	电化学的
semiconductor	半导体
photoelectric	光电的
IC＝integrated circuit	集成电路

- 词性转换较多

英语中的词性通常可以相互转换:名词可以转换为形容词或副词,形容词或副词也可以转换成名词;动词可转换为名词,名词和形容词也可以转换成动词,等等。这在其他西方语言中是罕见的。在科技英语文体中,这种转换表现尤为突出,许多技术名词都可以转换为同义的形容词。

1.2 Characteristics of Morphology
（词法的特点）

科技英语在词法方面的显著特点就是其名词化(nominalization)倾向。

- 广泛使用表示动作或状态的抽象名词,以及那些有名词功用的动名词

例如:

discovery of electromagnetic wave(＝to discover electromagnetic wave)　电磁波的

发现

standardization of the product(＝to standardize the product)　产品标准化
generation of electricity by friction(＝to generate electricity by friction)　摩擦生电

显然,运用这种动词名词化手段能有效简化叙事的层次和结构,减少使用句子和从句的频率,使行文更直接、紧凑和简洁。

- 广泛采用名词连用形式

名词连用现象在英语语法中称为"扩展的名词前置修饰语"(expanded noun premodifiers)。

例如:

oil pump	油泵
pressure difference	压力差
water pump valve	水泵阀
high voltage electrical energy	高压电能
room temperature	室温

很显然,名词连用可简化语言结构,使文章言简意赅。

- 普遍采用以名词为中心构成的词组来表达动词概念

例如:

make use of	利用
obtain support from	得到……支持
keep watch over	密切注视
give no evidence of	不足以说明

采用以名词为中心词构成的动词词组来表示动词概念,可使文中的谓语动词形式多样,增加行文的变化。

1.3　Characteristics of Syntax
　　（句法的特点）

- 广泛使用被动语态

和汉语相比,英语(包括其他西方语言)中被动语态用得更为普遍,再加上科技英语叙述的对象往往是事物、现象或过程,注重叙述客观事实,强调叙述的事物本身并不需要过多注意它的行为主体是什么,因此,使用被动语态不仅比较客观,而且可使读者的注意力集中在所叙述的客体上,便于集中精力对事物和现象进行分析和研究。

例如:

This kind of device is much needed in the speed-regulating system.
在调速系统中很需要这种装置。

- 较多使用长句

和汉语相比,英语中长句使用较多。在科技英语文体中,常常需要表达多重密切相关的概念,同时,科技英语文体又特别讲究推理严谨和叙述准确,因此,其句中修饰成分、限制成分和各种词组很多,这就必然形成长句。换句话说,长句的功能正好适应了科技英语文体的需要。

例如:

This chapter shall attempt to look at some aspects of controller synthesis for the multivariable servomechanism problem when the plant to be controlled is subject to uncertainty—in this case, a controller is to be found so that satisfactory regulation/tracking occurs in spite of the fact that the parameters of the plant may be allowed to vary (by arbitrary large amounts), subject only to the condition that the resultant perturbed system remains stable.

参考译文:本篇将致力于探讨在受控对象受到不确定性的影响时,多变量随动系统中控制器综合的某些方面的问题。在这种情况下,虽然受控对象的参数可能发生变化(变化可以任意大),但控制器仍具有令人满意的调节和跟随性能,只要系统受干扰后仍能保持稳定。

• 广泛使用包括非谓语动词短语在内的各种短语

如上所述,科技英语的句子较长,子句较多。但若子句太多,整个句子就会显得冗长。为使句子结构简洁,避免或减少复杂的长句,科技英语多采用各种类型的短语来代替子句。

例如:

Numerical control machines are most useful when quantities of products *to be produced* are low or mediocre; the tape *containing the information required to produce the part* can be stored, reused or modified *when required*.

参考译文:中小批量生产时,数控机床是极为有用的。其记录着零件生产的有关资料的磁带可储存起来以供下次使用,必要时还可修改。

上句并不算长,却使用了许多动词非限定形式,即非谓语动词短语,如句中斜体部分所示。非谓语动词短语在科技英语文体中运用之广泛,可见一斑。

1.4 Characteristics of Rhetoric
   (修辞的特点)

科技英语的修辞特点主要表现在时态的运用、修辞手法的选择和逻辑语法词的使用三个方面,具体特点分述如下。

• 时态运用有限

科技英语所运用的时态大都限于一般现在时、一般过去时、现在完成时和一般将来时这几种,其他时态运用相对较少。

(1) 一般现在时

科技英语中多使用一般现在时,主要是由于其常常需要对科学定义、定理、方程(或公式)以及图表等进行解说,这些客观真理性的内容是没有时间性的。此外,还时常有一些对通常发生或没有时限的自然现象、过程和常规等的表述,当其使用一般现在时时,给人以"无时间性"(timeless)的概念,以排除任何与时间关联的误解。因此可以说,一般现在时正是适应了这些"无时间性"的"一般陈述"(general statement)的需要。

（2）一般过去时和现在完成时

科技英语文体中常有叙述过去进行的研究的情况,若不与现在发生联系,常用一般过去时;若与现在关系直接且影响较大,则用现在完成时。

（3）一般将来时

当讨论计划中的项目研究时,科技英语文体均采用一般将来时,说明其为拟订中的活动。

- 修辞手法单调

与汉语一样,英语也有很多修辞手法。通常有夸张(hyperbole)、明喻(simile)、隐喻(metaphor)、借喻(metonymy)、拟人(personification)和对照(contrast)等。这些修辞手法在英语的文学体裁中是常见的,但在科技英语文体中却很少见,因为科技英语注重叙述事实和逻辑推理,若采用文学修辞法,会破坏科学的严肃性,弄巧成拙。

- 普遍使用逻辑性语法词

英语中的逻辑性语法词主要出现在科技英语文体中,其大体可分为以下几类:

① 表示原因的词,如 because of, due to, owing to, as, as a result of, caused by 等;

② 表示语气转折的词,如 but, however, nevertheless, yet, otherwise 等;

③ 表示逻辑顺序和顺理连接的词,如 so, thus, therefore, furthermore, moreover, in addition to 等;

④ 表示限制的词,如 only, if only, expect, besides, unless 等;

⑤ 表示假设的词,如 suppose, supposing, assuming, provided, providing 等。

1.5　Three Difficulties in Translation （译事三难）

从前面的分析可以看出,进行科技英语翻译,首先,要读懂英语原文;其次,要用汉语尽可能准确地加以表达。这就要求译者不仅要有一定的英语水平,而且要有汉语修养。不仅如此,由于我们所从事的是科技英语翻译,这就要求我们不仅对本专业的知识要有较好的掌握,而且应具备较宽的知识面。翻译界有一种说法叫"译事三难",具体到科技英语翻译,概括起来就是三句话:英语理解难、汉语表达难、专业知识要求高。

- 英语理解难

英语理解难,指的是要做好翻译,首先要看懂原文,这就要求译者有一定的英语水平。例如:

Scientific discoveries and inventions do not always influence the language in proportion to their importance.

有人译为:科学发现与发明就其重要性的比例而言,并不一定对语言有什么影响。

该译文的败笔,在于对英语词组 in proportion to 和 do not always 理解不透,致使译文与原文的意思有较大出入。in proportion to 是"按照……""根据……"的意思,而 do not always 是"并非总是"之意,因此原句直译应为:

科学发现和发明并不总是按照其重要性来影响语言的。

也可转译成：

科学发现与发明对语言的影响，并不取决于其重要性。

- 汉语表达难

汉语表达难，指的是看懂英文原文后，还要用地道的、规范的汉语表达出来，这就要求译者具有一定的汉语修养和语言文字表达水平。

例如：

A translator has to know everything of something and something of everything.

有人译为：

翻译人员对一些事情要什么都懂，对所有事情又要多少懂一些。

可以看出，译文虽与原文形似，但译者的汉语文字功底尚嫌不足，译文略欠文采。若译为：

翻译人员既要学问精深，又要知识广博。

就很精彩了。

- 专业知识要求高

专业知识要求高，指的是科技英语的译者，不仅要有较丰富的专业知识，还要有较宽的自然科学的知识面。这一点是科技英语译者与一般英语文体的译者所不同的地方。

Part 9

Signals

9.1 Introduction

Signals may describe a wide variety of physical phenomena. Although signals can be represented in many ways, in all cases the information in a signal is contained in a pattern of variations of some form[1].

Signals are represented mathematically as functions of one or more independent variables. For example, a speech signal can be represented mathematically by acoustic pressure as a function of time, and a picture can be represented by brightness as a function of two spatial variables. In this part, we focus our attention on signals involving a single independent variable. For convenience, we will generally refer to the independent variable as time, although it may not in fact represent time in specific applications. For example, in geophysics, signals representing variations with depth of physical quantities such as density, porosity, and electrical resistivity are used to study the structure of the earth. Also, knowledge of the variations of air pressure, temperature, and wind speed with altitude are extremely important in meteorological investigations. Throughout this part we will be considering two basic types of signals: continuous-time signals and discrete-time signals.

9.2 Continuous-Time and Discrete-Time Signals

In the case of continuous-time signals the independent variable is continuous, and thus these signals are defined for a continuum of values of the independent variable. On the other hand, discrete-time signals are defined only at discrete times, and consequently, for these signals, the independent variable takes on only a discrete set of values. A speech signal as a function of time and atmospheric pressure as a function of altitude are examples of continuous-time signals. Examples of discrete-time signals can be found in demographic studies in which various attributes, such as the average budget, crime rate, or pounds of fish caught, are tabulated against such discrete variables as family size, total population, or the type of fishing vessels, respectively.

To distinguish between continuous-time and discrete-time signals, we will use the *symbol* t to denote the continuous-time independent variable and n to denote the discrete time independent variable. In addition, for continuous-time signals we will enclose the independent variable in parentheses (•), whereas for discrete-time signals we will use brackets [•] to enclose the independent variable. We will also have frequent occasions when it will be useful to represent signals graphically. Illustrations of a continuous-time signal $x(t)$ and a discrete-time signal $x[n]$ are shown in Fig. 9.1. It is important to note that the discrete-time signal $x[n]$ is defined only for integer values of the independent variable. Our choice of graphical representation for $x[n]$ emphasizes this fact, and for further emphasis we will on occasion refer to $x[n]$ as a discrete-time sequence.

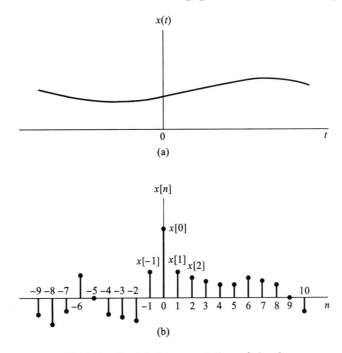

Fig. 9.1 Graphical representations of signals

(a) Continuous-time signals (b) Discrete-time signals

A discrete-time signal $x[n]$ may represent a phenomenon for which the independent variable is inherently discrete. Signals such as demographic data are examples of this. On the other hand, a very important class of discrete-time signals arises from the sampling of continuous-time signals. In this case, the discrete-time signal $x[n]$ represents successive samples of an underlying phenomenon for which the independent variable is continuous[2]. Because of their speed, computational power, and flexibility, modern digital processors are used to implement many practical systems, ranging from digital autopilots to digital audio systems. Such systems require the use of discrete-time sequences representing sampled versions of continuous-time signals—e. g. , aircraft position, velocity, and heading for an autopilot or speech and music for an audio system. Also, pictures in newspapers, for that matter—actually consist of a very fine grid of points, and each of these points represents a sample of the brightness of the corresponding point in the original image. No matter what the source of the data, however, the signal $x[n]$ is defined only for integer values of n. It makes no more sense to refer to the $3\frac{1}{2}$ sample of a digital speech signal than it does to refer to the average budget for a family with $2\frac{1}{2}$ family members.

9.3 Periodic Signals

An important class of signals that we will encounter frequently is the class of periodic signals. A periodic continuous-time signal $x(t)$ has the property that there is a positive value of T for which

$$x(t) = x(t+T) \tag{9.1}$$

for all values of t. In other words, a periodic signal has the property that it is unchanged by a time shift of T. In this case, we say that $x(t)$ is periodic with period T.

An example of a periodic continuous-time signal is given in Fig. 9.2. From the figure or from Eq. (9.1), we can readily deduce that if $x(t)$ is periodic with period T, then $x(t) = x(t+mT)$ for all t and for any integer m. Thus, $x(t)$ is also periodic with period $2T$, $3T$, $4T$, …. The fundamental period T_0 of $x(t)$ is the smallest positive value of T for which Eq. (9.1) holds. This definition of the fundamental period works, except if $x(t)$ is a constant. In this case the fundamental period is undefined, since $x(t)$ is periodic for any choice of T (so there is no smallest positive value)[3]. A signal $x(t)$ that is not periodic will be referred to as an aperiodic signal.

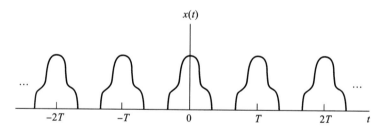

Fig. 9.2 A continuous-time periodic signal

Periodic signals are defined analogously in discrete time. Specifically, a discrete time signal $x[n]$ is periodic with period N, where N is a positive integer, if it is unchanged by a time shift of N, i.e., if

$$x[n] = x[n+N] \tag{9.2}$$

for all values of n. If Eq. (9.2) holds, then $x[n]$ is also periodic with period $2N$, $3N$, …. The fundamental period N_0 is the smallest positive value of N for which Eq. (9.2) holds. An example of a discrete-time periodic signal with fundamental period $N_0 = 3$ is shown in Fig. 9.3.

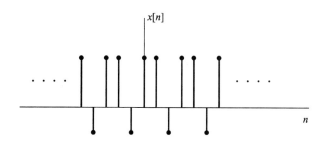

Fig. 9.3 A discrete-time periodic signal with fundamental period $N_0 = 3$

9.4 Even and Odd Signals

Another set of useful properties of signals relates to their symmetry under time reversal. A signal $x(t)$ or $x[n]$ is referred to as an even signal if it is identical to its time-reversed counterpart, i. e., with its reflection about the origin[4]. In continuous time a signal is even if

$$x(-t) = x(t) \tag{9.3}$$

while a discrete-time signal is even if

$$x[-n] = x[n] \tag{9.4}$$

A signal is referred to as odd if

$$x(-t) = -x(t) \tag{9.5}$$
$$x[-n] = -x[n] \tag{9.6}$$

An odd signal must necessarily be 0 at $t=0$ or $n=0$, since Eqs. (9.5) and (9.6) require that $x(0) = -x(0)$ and $x[0] = -x[0]$. Examples of even and odd continuous-time signals are shown in Fig. 9.4.

An important fact is that any signal can be broken into a sum of two signals, one of which is even and one of which is odd. To see this, consider the signal

$$\varepsilon_v\{x(t)\} = \frac{1}{2}[x(t) + x(-t)] \tag{9.7}$$

which is referred to as the even part of $x(t)$. Similarly, the odd part of $x(t)$ is given by

$$o_d\{x(t)\} = \frac{1}{2}[x(t) - x(-t)] \tag{9.8}$$

It is a simple exercise to check that the even part is in fact even, that the odd part is odd, and that $x(t)$ is the sum of the two. Exactly analogous definitions hold in the discrete-time case.

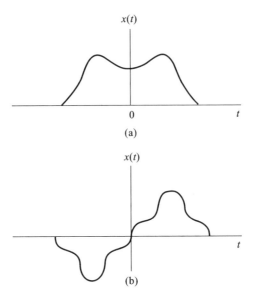

Fig. 9.4 Examples of even and odd continuous-time signals
(a) An even continuous-time signal (b) An odd continuous-time signal

9.5　The Unit Impulse and Unit Step Functions

In this section, we introduce several other basic signals—specifically, the unit impulse and step functions in continuous and discrete time—that are also of considerable importance in signal and system analysis. We begin with the discrete-time case.

9.5.1　The Discrete-Time Unit Impulse and Unit Step Sequences

One of the simplest discrete-time signals is the *unit impulse* (or *unit sample*), which is defined as

$$\delta[n] = \begin{cases} 0, n \neq 0 \\ 1, n = 0 \end{cases} \tag{9.9}$$

and which is shown in Fig. 9.5.

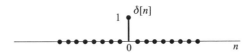

Fig. 9.5　Discrete-time unit impulse (sample)

A second basic discrete-time signal is the discrete-time *unit step*, denoted by $u[n]$ and defined by

$$u[n] = \begin{cases} 0, n < 0 \\ 1, n \geqslant 0 \end{cases} \tag{9.10}$$

The unit step sequence is shown in Fig. 9.6.

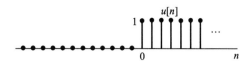

Fig. 9. 6 Discrete-time unit step sequence

There is a close relationship between the discrete-time unit impulse and unit step. In particular, the discrete-time unit impulse is the *first difference* of the discrete-time step

$$\delta[n] = u[n] - u[n-1] \tag{9.11}$$

Conversely, the discrete-time unit step is the *running sum* of the unit sample. That is,

$$u[n] = \sum_{m=-\infty}^{n} \delta[m] \tag{9.12}$$

Equation (9.12) is illustrated graphically in Fig. 9.7. Since the only nonzero value of the unit sample is at the point at which its argument is zero, we see from the figure that the running sum in Eq. (9.12) is 0 for $n \geqslant 0$.

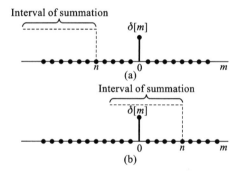

Fig. 9. 7 Running sum of Eq. (9.12)

(a) $n<0$ (b) $n>0$

9.5.2 The Continuous-Time Unit Step and Unit Impulse Functions

The continuous-time *unit step function* $u(t)$ is defined in a manner similar to its discrete-time counterpart. Specifically,

$$u(t) = \begin{cases} 0, t < 0 \\ 1, t > 0 \end{cases} \tag{9.13}$$

as is shown in Fig. 9.8. Note that the unit step is discontinuous at t_0. The continuous-time *unit impulse function* $\delta(t)$ is related to the unit step in a manner analogous to the relationship between the discrete-time unit impulse and step functions. In particular, the continuous-time unit step is the *running integral* of the unit impulse

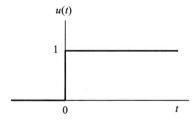

Fig. 9. 8 Continuous-time unit step function

$$u(t) = \int_{-\infty}^{t} \delta(\tau) d\tau \qquad (9.14)$$

This also suggests a relationship between $\delta(t)$ and $u(t)$ analogous to the expression for $\delta[n]$ in Eq. (9.11). In particular, it follows from Eq. (9.14) that the continuous-time unit impulse can be thought of as the *first derivative* of the continuous-time unit step:

$$\delta(t) = \frac{du(t)}{dt} \qquad (9.15)$$

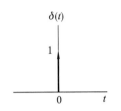

Fig. 9.9 Continuous-time unit impulse

Since $\delta(t)$ has, in effect, no duration but unit area, we adopt the graphical notation for it shown in Fig. 9.9, where the arrow at $t=0$ indicates that the area of the pulse is concentrated at $t=0$ and the height of the arrow and the "1" next to the arrow are used to represent the *area* of the impulse.

Although our discussion of the unit impulse in this section has been somewhat informal, it does provide us with some important intuition about this signal that will be useful. As we have stated, the unit impulse should be viewed as an idealization. Any real physical system has some inertia associated with it and thus does not respond instantaneously to inputs. Consequently, if a pulse of sufficiently short duration is applied to such a system, the system response will not be noticeably influenced by the pulse's duration or by the details of the shape of the pulse, for that matter. Instead, the primary characteristic of the pulse that will matter is the net, integrated effect of the pulse—i.e., its area[5]. For systems that respond much more quickly than others, the pulse will have to be of much shorter duration before the details of the pulse shape or its duration no longer matter. Nevertheless, for any physical system, we can always find a pulse that is "short enough". The unit impulse then is an idealization of this concept—the pulse that is short enough for *any* system. The response of a system to this idealized pulse plays a crucial role in signal and system analysis.

9.6 Summary

In this part, we have developed a number of basic concepts related to continuous-time and discrete-time signals. We also defined graphical and mathematical representations of several basic signals, both in continuous time and in discrete time. These included unit impulse and step functions. In addition, we investigated the concept of periodicity for continuous-time and discrete-time signals.

New Words and Expressions

1. acoustic *adj.* 声学的,听觉的
2. spatial *adj.* 空间的
3. geophysics *n.* 地球物理学
4. porosity *n.* 孔隙率,多孔性
5. meteorological *adj.* 气象的
6. demographic *adj.* 人口统计的
7. tabulate *v.* 把……制成表格
8. enclose *v.* 围绕,围住
9. parenthesis *n.* 圆括号
10. illustration *n.* 插图,说明
11. inherently *adv.* 内在地,固有地
12. autopilot *n.* 自动驾驶仪
13. heading *n.* 方向,标题
14. aperiodic *adj.* 非周期性的
15. analogously *adv.* 类似地,近似地
16. symmetry *n.* 对称(性)
17. reversal *n.* 逆转,反转
18. counterpart *n.* 对应物,副本
19. reflection *n.* 映像,投影
20. difference *n.* 差分,差异
21. running sum 运行总和,当前和
22. derivative *n.* 导数
23. duration *n.* 持续的时间,期间
24. intuition *n.* 直觉,直观
25. inertia *n.* 惯性,惰性
26. instantaneously *adv.* 即刻

Notes

1. Although signals can be represented in many ways, in all cases the information in a signal is contained in a pattern of variations of some form.

虽然信号可以用多种方式表示,但在所有情况下,信号中的信息都包含在某一形式的变异形态中。

2. In this case, the discrete-time signal $x[n]$ represents successive samples of an underlying phenomenon for which the independent variable is continuous.

在这种情况下,离散时间信号 $x[n]$ 代表对自变量是连续的底层事件的依次取样。

3. In this case the fundamental period is undefined, since $x(t)$ is periodic for any choice of T (so there is no smallest positive value).

当 $x(t)$ 为恒值时(承接上文的意思),基波周期的定义是不成立的,因为对任意 T 值 $x(t)$ 都是周期性的(所以不存在正的最小周期)。

4. A signal $x(t)$ or $x[n]$ is referred to as an even signal if it is identical to its time-reversed counterpart, i.e., with its reflection about the origin.

如果信号 $x(t)$ 或 $x[n]$ 与时间取反后对应的信号相同,也就是 $x(t)$ 或 $x[n]$ 存在关于原点的倒影,则称其为偶信号。

5. Instead, the primary characteristic of the pulse that will matter is the net, integrated effect of the pulse—i.e., its area.

相反，脉冲的主要特征是指脉冲的有效及综合效应，也就是脉冲的面积。

Exercises

I. Translate the phrases into English.

1. 自变量 2. 语音信号 3. 密度 4. 连续时间信号
5. 离散时间信号 6. 整数 7. 序列 8. 依次取样
9. 速度 10. 网格 11. 亮度 12. 周期信号
13. 基波周期 14. 偶信号 15. 奇信号 16. 单位脉冲
17. 单位阶跃 18. 函数 19. 一阶差分 20. 导数
21. 积分 22. 响应 23. 周期性

II. Answer the following questions according to the text.

1. What kind of values does the independent variable take on for discrete-time signals?
2. How to denote the continuous-time and discrete-time independent variables?
3. What is the property of a periodic signal?
4. How to define an even signal and an odd signal?
5. Why doesn't a real physical system respond instantaneously to inputs?

III. Translate the sentences into Chinese.

1. In the case of continuous-time signals the independent variable is continuous, and thus these signals are defined for a continuum of values of the independent variable.

2. Specifically, a discrete-time signal $x[n]$ is periodic with period N, where N is a positive integer, if it is unchanged by a time shift of N.

3. An important fact is that any signal can be broken into a sum of two signals, one of which is even and one of which is odd.

4. In particular, the discrete-time unit impulse is the *first difference* of the discrete-time step. Conversely, the discrete-time unit step is the *running sum* of the unit sample.

5. The continuous-time unit step is the *running integral* of the unit impulse. The continuous-time unit impulse can be thought of as the *first derivative* of the continuous-time unit step.

6. The unit impulse then is an idealization of this concept—the pulse that is short enough for any system.

Part 10

Continuous-Time and Discrete-Time Systems

10.1 Introduction

Physical systems in the broadest sense are an interconnection of components, devices, or subsystems. In contexts ranging from signal processing and communications to electromechanical motors, automotive vehicles, and chemical-processing plants, a *system* can be viewed as a process in which input signals are transformed by the system or cause the system to respond in some way, resulting in other signals as output. For example, a high-fidelity system takes a recorded audio signal and generates a reproduction of that signal. If the hi-fi system has tone controls, we can change the tonal quality of the reproduced signal.

A *continuous-time system* is a system in which continuous-time input signals are applied and result in continuous-time output signals. Such a system will be represented pictorially as in Fig. 10.1(a), where $x(t)$ is the input and $y(t)$ is the output. Alternatively, we will often represent the input-output relation of a continuous-time system by the notation $x(t) \rightarrow y(t)$.

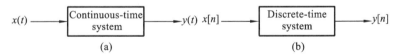

Fig. 10.1 Diagram of a system

(a) Continuous-time system (b) Discrete-time system

Similarly, a *discrete-time system*—that is, a system that transforms discrete-time inputs into discrete-time outputs—will be depicted as in Fig. 10.1(b) and will sometimes be represented symbolically as $x[n] \rightarrow y[n]$.

10.2 Interconnections of Systems

Many real systems are built as interconnections of several subsystems. By viewing such a system as an interconnection of its components, we can use our understanding of the component systems and of how they are interconnected in order to analyze the operation and behavior of the overall system. In addition, by describing a system in terms of an interconnection of simpler subsystems, we may in fact be able to define useful ways in which to synthesize complex systems out of simpler, basic building blocks[1].

While one can construct a variety of system interconnections, there are several basic ones that are frequently encountered. A *series* or *cascade interconnection* of two systems is illustrated in Fig. 10.2(a). Diagrams such as this are referred to as *block diagrams*. Here, the output of System 1 is the input to System 2, and the overall system transforms an input by processing it first by System 1 and then by System 2. An example of a series interconnection is a radio receiver followed by an amplifier. Similarly, one can define a series interconnection of three or more systems.

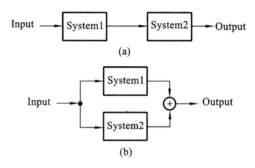

Fig. 10.2 Interconnection of two systems

(a) Series (cascade) interconnection (b) Parallel interconnection

A *parallel interconnection* of two systems is illustrated in Fig. 10.2(b). Here, the same input signal is applied to Systems 1 and 2. The symbol "⊕" in the figure denotes addition, so that the output of the parallel interconnection is the sum of the outputs of Systems 1 and 2. An example of a parallel interconnection is a simple audio system with several microphones feeding into a single amplifier and speaker system. In addition to the simple parallel interconnection in Fig. 10.2(b), we can define parallel interconnections of more than two systems, and we can combine both cascade and parallel interconnections to obtain more complicated interconnections.

Another important type of system interconnection is a *feedback interconnection*, an example of which is illustrated in Fig. 10.3. Here, the output of System 1 is the input to System 2, while the output of System 2 is fed back and added to the external input to produce the actual input to System 1. Feedback systems arise in a wide variety of applications. For example, a cruise control system on an automobile senses the vehicle's velocity and adjusts the fuel flow in order to keep the speed at the desired level. Similarly, a digitally controlled aircraft is most naturally thought of as a feedback system in which differences between actual and desired speed, heading, or altitude are fed back through the autopilot in order to correct these discrepancies.

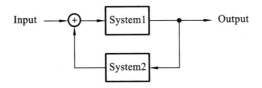

Fig. 10.3 Feedback interconnection

10.3 Basic System Properties

In this section we introduce and discuss a number of basic properties of continuous-time and discrete-time systems. These properties have important physical interpretations and relatively simple mathematical descriptions using the signals and systems language that we have begun to develop.

10.3.1 Systems with and without Memory

A system is said to be *memoryless* if its output for each value of the independent variable at a given time is dependent only on the input at that same time. For example, the system specified by the relationship

$$y[n] = (2x[n] - x^2[n])^2 \tag{10.1}$$

is memoryless, as the value of $y[n]$ at any particular time n_0 depends only on the value of $x[n]$ at that time. Similarly, a resistor is a memoryless system; with the input $x(t)$ taken as the current and with the voltage taken as the output $y(t)$, the input-output relationship of a resistor is

$$y(t) = Rx(t) \tag{10.2}$$

where R is the resistance.

An example of a discrete-time system with memory is an *accumulator*

$$y[n] = \sum_{k=-\infty}^{n} x[k] \tag{10.3}$$

and a second example is a *delay*

$$y[n] = x[n-1] \tag{10.4}$$

A capacitor is an example of a continuous-time system with memory, since if the input is taken to be the current and the output is the voltage, then

$$y(t) = \frac{1}{C}\int_{-\infty}^{t} x(\tau)\,d\tau \tag{10.5}$$

where C is the capacitance.

In many physical systems, memory is directly associated with the storage of energy. For example, the capacitor in Eq. (10.5) stores energy by accumulating electric charge, represented as the integral of the current. In discrete-time systems implemented with computers or digital microprocessors, memory is typically directly associated with storage registers that retain values between clock pulses.

While the concept of memory in a system would typically suggest storing *past* input and output values, our formal definition also leads to our referring to a system as having memory if the current output is dependent on *future* values of the input and output[2]. While systems having this dependence on future values might at first seem unnatural, they in fact form an important class of systems.

10.3.2 Causality

A system is *causal* if the output at any time depends only on values of the input at the present time and in the past. Such a system is often referred to as being *nonanticipative*, as the system output does not anticipate future values of the input[3]. Consequently, if two inputs to a causal system are identical up to some point in time t_0 or n_0, the corresponding outputs must also be equal up to this same time. The motion of an automobile is causal, since it does not anticipate future actions of the driver. The systems described in Eqs. (10.3)-(10.5) are also causal, but the systems defined by

$$y[n] = x[n] - x[n+1] \qquad (10.6)$$

and

$$y(t) = x(t+1) \qquad (10.7)$$

are not. All memoryless systems are causal, since the output responds only to the current value of the input.

Although causal systems are of great importance, they do not by any means constitute the only systems that are of practical significance. For example, causality is not often an essential constraint in applications in which the independent variable is not time, such as in image processing. Furthermore, in processing data that have been recorded previously, as often happens with speech, geophysical, or meteorological signals, to name a few, we are by no means constrained to causal processing.

10.3.3 Stability

Stability is another important system property. Informally, a stable system is one in which small inputs lead to responses that do not diverge. For example, consider the pendulum in Fig. 10.4(a), in which the input is the applied force $x(t)$ and the output is the angular deviation $y(t)$ from the vertical. In this case, gravity applies a restoring force that tends to return the pendulum to the vertical position, and frictional losses due to drag tend to slow it down. Consequently, if a small force $x(t)$ is applied, the resulting deflection from vertical will also be small. In contrast, for the inverted pendulum in Fig. 10.4(b), the effect of gravity is to apply a force that tends to *increase* the deviation from vertical. Thus, a small applied force leads to a large vertical deflection causing the pendulum to topple over, despite any retarding forces due to friction[4].

The system in Fig. 10.4(a) is an example of a stable system, while that in Fig. 10.4

(b) is unstable.

The preceding examples provide us with an intuitive understanding of the concept of stability. More formally, if the input to a stable system is bounded (i. e. , if its magnitude does not grow without bound), then the output must also be bounded and therefore cannot diverge. This is a kind of the definition of stability.

10.3.4 Time Invariance

Conceptually, a system is time invariant if the behavior and characteristics of the system are fixed over time.

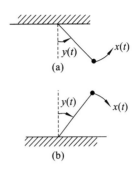

Fig. 10. 4   Different pendulums
(a) A stable pendulum
(b) An unstable inverted pendulum

The property of time invariance can be described very simply in terms of the signals and systems language. Specifically, a system is time invariant if a time shift in the input signal results in an identical time shift in the output signal. That is, if $y[n]$ is the output of a discrete-time, time-invariant system when $x[n]$ is the input, then $y[n-n_0]$ is the output when $x[n-n_0]$ is applied. In continuous time with $y(t)$ the output corresponding to the input $x(t)$, a time-invariant system will have $y(t-t_0)$ as the output when $x(t-t_0)$ is the input.

10.3.5 Linearity

A *linear system*, in continuous time or discrete time, is a system that possesses the important property of superposition: If an input consists of the weighted sum of several signals, then the output is the superposition—that is, the weighted sum—of the responses of the system to each of those signals[5]. More precisely, let $y_1(t)$ be the response of a continuous-time system to an input $x_1(t)$, and let $y_2(t)$ be the output corresponding to the input $x_2(t)$. Then the system is linear if:

① The response to $x_1(t)+x_2(t)$ is $y_1(t)+y_2(t)$.

② The response to $ax_1(t)$ is $ay_1(t)$, where a is any complex constant.

The first of these two properties is known as the *additivity* property; the second is known as the *scaling* or *homogeneity* property. Although we have written this description using continuous-time signals, the same definition holds in discrete time. The systems specified by Eqs. (10. 2)-(10. 7) are linear, while that defined by Eq. (10. 1) is nonlinear.

continuous time: $ax_1(t)+bx_2(t) \to ay_1(t)+by_2(t)$ (10. 8)

discrete time: $ax_1[n]+bx_2[n] \to ay_1[n]+by_2[n]$ (10. 9)

Here, a and b are any complex constants. Furthermore, it is straightforward to show from the definition of linearity that if $x_k[n]$, $k=1, 2, 3, \ldots$, are a set of inputs to a discrete-time linear system with corresponding outputs $y_k[n]$, $k=1, 2, 3, \ldots$, then the response to a linear combination of these inputs given by

$$x[n] = \sum_k a_k x_k[n] = a_1 x_1[n] + a_2 x_2[n] + a_3 x_3[n] + \ldots \quad (10. 10)$$

is
$$y[n] = \sum_k a_k y_k[n] = a_1 y_1[n] + a_2 y_2[n] + a_3 y_3[n] + \ldots \qquad (10.11)$$

This very important fact is known as the *superposition property*, which holds for linear systems in both continuous and discrete time.

10.4 Summary

In this part, we have developed a number of basic concepts related to continuous-time and discrete-time systems. We introduced block diagrams to facilitate our discussions concerning the interconnection of systems, and we defined a number of important properties of systems, including memory, causality, stability, time invariance, and linearity.

New Words and Expressions

1. electromechanical *adj.* 机电的
2. fidelity *n.* 保真度,忠诚
3. tonal *adj.* 音调的,色调的
4. pictorially *adv.* 以图片的方式
5. alternatively *adv.* 或者,要不
6. notation *n.* 符号,记法
7. depict *v.* 描述,描画
8. symbolically *adv.* 符号化
9. synthesize *v.* 合成,综合
10. cascade *n.* 串联
11. audio *adj.* 音频的,声音的
12. speaker *n.* 扬声器
13. cruise *n.* 巡航,巡游
14. discrepancy *n.* 差异,矛盾
15. interpretation *n.* 解释,翻译
16. retain *v.* 保持,保留
17. constraint *n.* 约束,强制
18. diverge *v.* 偏离,分歧
19. pendulum *n.* 摆,钟摆
20. deflection *n.* 偏向,偏差
21. topple *v.* 倾倒,摇摇欲坠
22. retard *v.* 延迟,阻止
23. superposition *n.* 叠加,重合
24. additivity *n.* 可加性,相加性
25. scaling *n.* 缩放,缩放比例
26. homogeneity *n.* 同质,齐次性

Notes

1. In addition, by describing a system in terms of an interconnection of simpler subsystems, we may in fact be able to define useful ways in which to synthesize complex systems out of simpler, basic building blocks.

此外,我们通过用简单子系统的相互连接来描述一个系统,实际上就可能得出用简单、基础的构件合成复杂系统的方法。

2. While the concept of memory in a system would typically suggest storing *past* input

and output values, our formal definition also leads to our referring to a system as having memory if the current output is dependent on *future* values of the input and output.

系统中记忆的概念通常会使人联想到存储的输入和输出的过去值,但正式的定义为:如果当前的输出与输入和输出的将来值有关,那么我们称系统是具有记忆的。

3. Such a system is often referred to as being *nonanticipative*, as the system output does not anticipate future values of the input.

这种系统通常被称为非预期的,因为系统输出不会预测出输入的将来值。

4. Thus, a small applied force leads to a large vertical deflection causing the pendulum to topple over, despite any retarding forces due to friction.

因此,尽管存在因摩擦而产生的阻力,但一个小的作用力就会引起钟摆大的垂直偏转,从而导致钟摆倒下。

5. If an input consists of the weighted sum of several signals, then the output is the superposition—that is, the weighted sum—of the responses of the system to each of those signals.

如果输入由几个信号的加权和组成,那么输出就是系统对每个输入信号响应的叠加即加权和。

Exercises

I. Translate the phrases into English.

1. 高保真　　2. 串联　　3. 方框图　　4. 并联　　5. 反馈
6. 累加器　　7. 延时　　8. 时钟脉冲　　9. 因果关系　　10. 稳定性
11. 发散　　12. 时不变　　13. 稳定系统　　14. 不稳定的　　15. 非线性
16. 叠加　　17. 复常数　　18. 相加性　　19. 缩放　　20. 齐次性

II. Answer the following questions according to the text.

1. How to describe a series or parallel interconnection of two systems?
2. Please list an example of a continuous-time system with or without memory from this part.
3. Why are all memoryless systems causal?
4. How will responses of the system change when small input is applied to an unstable system?
5. What are the two properties of the linear system?

III. Translate the sentences into Chinese.

1. Physical systems in the broadest sense are an interconnection of components, devices, or subsystems.
2. A *system* can be viewed as a process in which input signals are transformed by the system or cause the system to respond in some way, resulting in other signals as outputs.
3. The output of System 1 is the input to System 2, while the output of System 2 is

fed back and added to the external input to produce the actual input to System 1.

4. A system is said to be *memoryless* if its output for each value of the independent variable at a given time is dependent only on the input at that same time.

5. A system is *causal* if the output at any time depends only on values of the input at the present time and in the past.

6. More formally, if the input to a stable system is bounded (i. e. , if its magnitude does not grow without bound), then the output must also be bounded and therefore cannot diverge.

7. A system is time invariant if a time shift in the input signal results in an identical time shift in the output signal.

8. A linear system, in continuous time or discrete time, is a system that possesses the important property of superposition.

Part 11

Automatic Control Systems

11.1 Introduction

Control systems are everywhere around us and within us. Many complex control systems are included among the functions of the human body[1]. Threading a needle and driving an automobile are two ways in which the human body functions as a complex controller. The eyes are the sensor that detects the position of the needle and thread or of the automobile and the center of the load. A complex controller, the brain, compares the two positions and determines which actions must be performed to accomplish the desired result. The body implements the control action by moving the thread or turning the steering wheel; an experienced driver will anticipate all types of disturbances to the system, such as a rough section of pavement or a slow-moving vehicle ahead. It would be very difficult to reproduce in an automatic controller the many judgments that an average person makes daily and unconsciously.

A *control system* is any group of components that maintains a desired result or value. It is clear that a great variety of components may be a part of a single control system, whether they are electrical, electronic, mechanical, hydraulic, pneumatic, human, or any combination of these. The desired result is a value of some variables in the system, for example, the direction of an automobile, the temperature of a room, the level of liquid in a tank, or the pressure in a pipe. The variable whose value is controlled is called the *controlled variable*.

To achieve control, there must be another variable in the system that can influence the controlled variable. Most systems have several such variables. The control system maintains the desired result by manipulating the value of one of these influential variables. The variable that is manipulated is called the *manipulated variable*. The steering wheel of an automobile is an example of a manipulated variable.

As stated above, a control system is a group of components that maintains a desired result by manipulating the value of another variable in the system.

11.2 Block Diagrams and Transfer Functions

Although it is not unusual to find several kinds of components in a single control system, or two systems with completely different kinds of components, any control system can be described by a set of mathematical equations that define the characteristics of each component. A wide range of control problems—including processes, machine tools, servomechanisms, space vehicles, traffic, and even economics—can be analyzed by the same mathematical methods. The important feature of each component is the effect it has on the system. The *block diagram* is a method of representing a control system that retains only this important feature of each component. *Signal lines* indicate the input and output signals of the component, as shown in Fig. 11.1. In Fig. 11.1, the energy source is not shown on most block diagrams. However, many components do have an external energy source that makes amplification of the input signal possible.

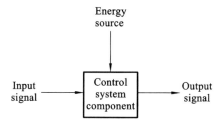

Fig. 11.1 Block representation of a component

Each component receives an input signal from some part of the system and produces an output signal for another part of the system. The signals can be electric current, voltage, air pressure, liquid flow rate, liquid pressure, temperature, speed, acceleration, position, direction, or others. The signal paths can be electric wires, pneumatic tubes, hydraulic lines, mechanical linkages, or anything that transfers a signal from one component to another. The component may use some source of energy to increase the power of the output signal. Figure 11.2 illustrates block representations of the automobile.

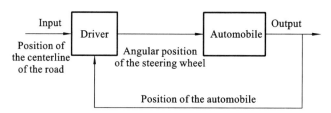

Fig. 11.2 Simplified block diagram of a person driving an automobile

11.2.1 Block Diagrams

A block diagram consists of a block representing each component in a control system connected by lines that represent the signal paths[2]. In Fig. 11.2 the driver's sense of sight provides the two input signals: the position of the automobile and the position of the center of the road. The driver compares the two positions and determines the position of the steering wheel that will maintain the proper position of the automobile. To implement the decision, the driver's hands and arms move the steering wheel to the new position. The automobile responds to the change in the steering wheel position with a corresponding change in direction. After a short time has elapsed, the new direction moves the automobile to a new position. Thus, there is a time delay between a change in position of the steering wheel and the change in the position of the automobile. This time delay is included in the mathematical equation of the block representing the automobile.

The loop in the block diagram indicates a fundamental concept of control. The actual position of the automobile is used to determine the correction necessary to maintain the desired position. This concept is called *feedback*, and control systems with feedback are called *closed-loop control systems*. Control systems that do not have feedback are called *open-loop control systems*, because their block diagram does not have a loop and the actual condition is not used to determine a corrective action.

11.2.2 Transfer Functions

The most important characteristic of a component is the relationship between the input signal and the output signal. This relationship is expressed by the *transfer function* of the component, which is defined as the ratio of the output signal divided by the input signal (Mostly, it is the Laplace transform of the output signal divided by the Laplace transform of the input signal).

The transfer function consists of two parts. One part is the *size* relationship between the input and the output. The other part is the *timing* between the input and output. For example, the size relationship may be such that the output is twice (or half) as large as the input, and the timing relationship may be such that there is a delay of 2 seconds between a change in the input and the corresponding change in the output.

If the component is linear and the input is a sinusoidal signal, then the output will also be a sinusoidal signal. The size relationship between the input and the output is measured by the ratio of the amplitude of the output signal divided by the amplitude of the input signal. We call this ratio the *gain* of the component. The phase difference of the component is the phase angle of the output signal minus the phase angle of the input signal. Thus the transfer function is represented by the complex number whose magnitude is the gain of the component and whose angle is the phase of the output minus the phase of the input.

The transfer function of a component describes the size and timing relationship between the output signal and the input signal.

11.3 Open-Loop Control

An open-loop control system does not compare the actual result with the desired result to determine the control action. Instead, a calibrated setting—previously determined by some sort of calibration procedure or calculation—is used to obtain the desired result.

The firing of a rifle bullet is an example of an open-loop control system. The desired result is to direct the bullet to the bull's-eye. The actual result is the direction of the bullet after the gun has been fired. The open-loop control occurs when the rifle is aimed at the bull's-eye and the trigger is pulled. Once the bullet leaves the barrel, it is on its own: If a sudden gust of wind comes up, the direction will change and no correction will be possible.

The primary advantage of open-loop control is that it is less expensive than closed-loop control: It is not necessary to measure the actual result. In addition, the controller is much simpler because a corrective action based on the error is not required. The disadvantage of open-loop control is that errors caused by unexpected disturbances are not corrected. Often a human operator must correct slowly changing disturbances by manual adjustment. In this case, the operator is actually closing the loop by providing the feedback signal.

11.4 Closed-Loop Control: Feedback

Feedback is the action of measuring the difference between the actual result and the desired result, and using that difference to drive the actual result toward the desired result. The term *feedback* comes from the direction in which the measured value signal travels in the block diagram. The signal begins at the output of the controlled system and ends at the input to the controller. The output of the controller is the input to the controlled system. Thus the measured value signal is fed back from the output of the controlled system to the input. The term *closed loop* refers to the loop created by the *feedback* path.

Block diagrams of closed-loop control systems are shown in Fig. 11.3, which is used in the design of process control systems. The names of the components and variables are used to other control systems. The *process block* represents everything performed in and by the equipment in which a variable is controlled[3]. The process includes everything that affects the controlled or *process variable* except the controller and the final control element. The *measuring transmitter*, or *sensor*, senses the value of the controlled variable and converts it into a usable signal. Although the measuring transmitter is considered as one block, it usually consists of a primary sensing element and a signal transducer (or signal converter). The term *measuring transmitter* is a general term to cover all types of signals. The controller includes the error detector and a unit that implements the control modes. The *error detector* computes the difference between the measured value of the controlled variable and the desired value (or set point). The difference E is called the *error* (i.e., $E=SP-C_m$). The *control modes* convert the error into a control action or *controller output* that will tend to reduce the error. The three most common control modes are the proportional mode (P), the integral mode (I), and the derivative mode (D). The *proportional mode* may be used alone or in combination with either or both of the other two modes. The *integral mode* can be used alone, but it almost never is. The *derivative mode* cannot be used alone. Thus the common control mode combinations are: P, PI, PD, and PID. The *manipulating element* uses the controller output to regulate the manipulated variable. Valves, dampers, fans, pumps, and heating elements are examples of manipulating elements.

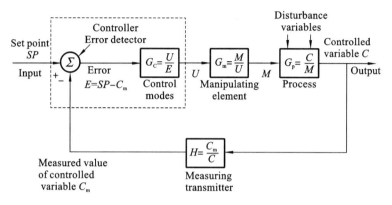

Fig. 11.3 Block diagram of a closed-loop process control system

A feedback control system performs the following operations: measurement, decision and manipulation. The measurement operation measures the value of the controlled variable. The decision operation computes the error (desired value minus measured value) and uses the error to form a control action. The manipulation operation uses the control action to manipulate some variable in the process in a way that will tend to reduce the error.

In Fig. 11.3, the set point (SP) is the input to the process control system, and the controlled variable (C) is the output. The feedback path consists of one component, the measuring transmitter with transfer function H. The forward path consists of three components (the control modes, the manipulating element, and the process) with transfer functions G_c, G_m, and G_p, respectively. The overall forward transfer function (G) is the product of the three component transfer functions:

$$G = G_c G_m G_p \tag{11.1}$$

The performance of a control system is usually based on a comparison between the set point (SP) and the measured value of the controlled variable (C_m). The reason C_m is used instead of C is that C_m is measurable and available, but C is not. We can derive the transfer function, C_m/SP, of the closed-loop process control system:

$$\frac{C_m}{SP} = \frac{GH}{1+GH} \tag{11.2}$$

11.5 Objectives of a Control System

At first glance, the objective of a control system seems quite simple—to maintain the controlled variable exactly equal to the set point at all times, regardless of load changes or set point changes. To do this, the control system must respond to a change before the error occurs; but unfortunately, feedback is never perfect because it does not act until an error occurs. First, a load change must change the controlled variable; this produces an error. Then the controller acts on the error to produce a change in the manipulated variable. Finally, the change in the manipulated variable drives the controlled variable back toward the set point[4].

It is more realistic for us to expect a control system to obtain as nearly perfect operation as possible. Because the errors in a control system occur after load changes and set point changes, it seems natural to define the objectives in terms of the response to such changes. Figure 11.4 shows a typical response of the controlled variable to a step change in load.

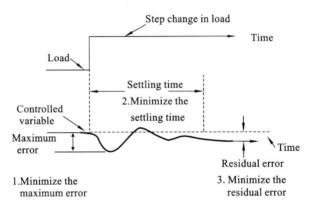

Fig. 11.4 Three objectives of a closed-loop control system

One obvious objective is to minimize the maximum value of the error signal. Some control systems (with an integral mode) will eventually reduce the error to zero, whereas others require a residual error to compensate for a load change. In either case, the control system should eventually return the error to a steady, unchanging value. The time required to accomplish this is called the *settling time*. A second objective of a control system is to minimize the settling time. A third objective is to minimize the *residual error* after setting out.

Unfortunately, these three objectives tend to be incompatible. For instance, the problem of reducing the residual error can be solved by increasing the gain of the controller so that a smaller residual error is required to produce the necessary corrective control action. However, an increase in gain tends to increase the settling time and may increase the maximum value of the error as well. The optimum response is always achieved through some sort of compromise.

New Words and Expressions

1. thread *v.* 穿过 *n.* 线
2. needle *n.* 针
3. anticipate *v.* 预见，预料
4. rough *adj.* 粗糙的
5. pavement *n.* 路面，人行道
6. unconsciously *adv.* 无意识地
7. hydraulic *adj.* 液压的，水力的
8. pneumatic *adj.* 气动的，充气的
9. manipulate *v.* 操作，巧妙地处理
10. define *v.* 定义，使明确
11. machine tool 机床
12. servomechanism *n.* 伺服机构
13. space vehicle 航天器，宇宙飞船
14. retain *v.* 保留，保持
15. line *n.* 路线，线
16. acceleration *n.* 加速度
17. sense of sight 视觉
18. elapse *v.* 时间过去，消逝
19. correction *n.* 修正，校正
20. calibrate *v.* 校正，校准
21. rifle *n.* 步枪
22. bull *n.* 靶心，公牛
23. trigger *n.* 扳机，触发器
24. transmitter *n.* 发送器，变送器
25. transducer *n.* 传感器，变换器
26. damper *n.* 阻尼器，气闸，风门
27. residual *adj.* 剩余的，残留的
28. compensate *v.* 补偿
29. set out 开始，测定
30. incompatible *adj.* 矛盾的
31. optimum *adj.* 最佳的，最适宜的
32. compromise *n.* 妥协，折中

Notes

1. Many complex control systems are included among the functions of the human body.

人体的功能包含许多复杂的控制系统。

2. A block diagram consists of a block representing each component in a control system connected by lines that represent the signal paths.

方框图由代表控制系统各个元件的方框组成，这些方框由代表信号通路的线段连接。

3. The process block represents everything performed in and by the equipment in which a variable is controlled.

过程方框代表被控变量所在装置完成的每件事或通过装置执行的每件事。

4. Finally, the change in the manipulated variable drives the controlled variable back toward the set point.

最后，控制量的改变带动被控变量向设定值方向变化。

Exercises

I. Translate the phrases into English.

1. 自动控制　　2. 控制器　　3. 扰动　　4. 期望值　　5. 压力
6. 液位　　　　7. 被控量　　8. 方框图　9. 传递函数　10. 过程控制
11. 伺服系统　 12. 流率　　 13. 加速度　14. 前向通路　15. 补偿
16. 反馈通路　 17. 闭环　　 18. 开环　　19. 输出　　　20. 增益
21. 手动调节　 22. 变送器　 23. 误差　　24. 控制方式　25. 比例控制
26. 积分控制　 27. 微分控制 28. 执行元件 29. 调节时间　30. 残差

II. Answer the following questions according to the text.

1. What is a control system?
2. How to define the transfer function?
3. If the component is linear and the input is a sinusoidal signal, what will the output be?
4. What is the gain of the component?
5. What are the advantages of open-loop control?
6. What can the error detector do?
7. How many common control modes are there? What are they?
8. What is the objective of a control system?

III. Translate the sentences into Chinese.

1. The transfer function of a component describes the size and timing relationship between the output signal and the input signal.

2. Feedback is the action of measuring the difference between the actual result and the desired result, and using that difference to drive the actual result toward the desired result.

3. The measuring transmitter, or sensor, senses the value of the controlled variable and converts it into a usable signal.

4. The decision operation computes the error (desired value minus measured value) and uses the error to form a control action. The manipulation operation uses the control action to manipulate some variable in the process in a way that will tend to reduce the error.

5. The problem of reducing the residual error can be solved by increasing the gain of the controlled so that a smaller residual error is required to produce the necessary corrective control action.

Part 12

Measurement

12.1 Introduction

A feedback control system performs three operations: measurement, decision, and manipulation. The measuring transmitter performs the measurement operation, the controller performs the decision operation, and the manipulating element performs the manipulation operation. Measurement is an essential operation in a feedback control system. In order to control a variable, we must first measure its value. Next, we must convert the measured value into a usable signal. Only then can the controller and the manipulating element perform their tasks. The controller cannot make a decision without the measured value of the controlled variable. The manipulating element does not know how to act without a decision from the controller. Feedback control begins with the measurement operation.

The purpose of a measuring instrument is to obtain the true value of the measured variable. The ideal measuring instrument would do this exactly, but in practice, this ideal is never achieved. There is always some uncertainty in the measurement of a variable. Indeed, there is even some uncertainty in the standards we use to calibrate a measuring instrument. For this reason, we begin the part with a brief review of statistics, the subject that deals with uncertainty.

12.2 Statistics

There is an uncertainty when we measure the value of a variable. This uncertainty occurs when repeated measurements under identical conditions give different results. For example, let's assume that five measurements of the temperature of a fluid result in the following measured values: 207, 204, 205, 205, and 206 ℃. Statistics cannot tell us what the true temperature is, but it can help us understand the uncertainty we are confronted with.

The individual measurements of a variable are called *observations*, and the entire collection of observations is called a *sample*. The simplest statistical measure of the sample is the *arithmetic average* or *mean*. The sample mean is an estimate of the expected value of the next observation. The mean is computed by summing the observations and dividing by the number of observations. The mean of a sample of n observations is given by the following equation:

$$\text{Sample mean } \bar{x} = \frac{x_1 + x_2 + x_3 + \cdots + x_n}{n} \tag{12.1}$$

The mean gives us an estimate of the expected value of an observation, but it gives no idea of the dispersion or variability of the observations[1]. For a measure of variability, we begin by computing the deviation between each observation and the mean.

$$\text{Deviation of observation } x_i = d_i = x_i - \bar{x}$$

The standard deviation, S_x, is a measure of variability, which is defined by the following equation:

$$S_x = \sqrt{\frac{d_1^2 + d_2^2 + d_3^2 + \cdots + d_n^2}{n-1}} \tag{12.2}$$

The standard deviation gives us an idea of the variability of the observations in the sample. If the errors in measurement are truly random and we take a large number of observations, 68% of all observations will be within 1 standard deviation of the mean. Over 95% of all samples will be within 2 standard deviations of the mean, and almost all samples will be within 3 standard deviations of the mean.

12.3 Operating Characteristics

Operating characteristics include details about the measurement by, and operation of effects on the measuring instrument[2].

12.3.1 Measurement

A measuring instrument can measure any value of a variable within its *range* of measurement. The range is defined by the *lower range limit* and the *upper range limit*. As the names imply, the range consists of all values between the lower range limit and the upper range limit. The *span* is the difference between the upper range limit and the lower range limit.

$$\text{Span} = \text{upper range limit} - \text{lower range limit}$$

Resolution, dead band, and sensitivity are different characteristics that relate in different ways to an increment of measurement[3]. When the measured variable is continuously varied over the range, some measuring instruments change their output in discrete steps rather than in a continuous manner. The *resolution* of this type of measuring instrument is a single step of the output. Resolution is usually expressed as a percentage of the output span of the instrument. Sometimes the size of the steps varies through the range of the instrument. In this case, the largest step is the *maximum resolution*. The *average resolution*, expressed as a percentage of output span, is 100 divided by the total number of steps over the range of the instrument.

$$\text{Average resolution } (\%) = \frac{100}{N} \tag{12.3}$$

where N represents the total number of steps.

The *dead band* of a measuring instrument is the smallest change in the measured variable that will result in a measurable change in the output. Obviously, a measuring instrument cannot measure changes in the measured variable that are smaller than its dead band. *Threshold* is another name for *dead band*.

The *sensitivity* of a measuring instrument is the ratio of the change in output divided by the change in the input that caused the change in output. Sensitivity and gain are both defined as a change in output divided by the corresponding change in input. However, *sensitivity* refers to static values, whereas *gain* usually refers to the amplitude of sinusoidal signals.

12.3.2 Operation

The *reliability* of a measuring instrument is the probability that it will do its job for a specified period of time under a specified set of conditions. The conditions include limits on the operating environment, the amount of overrange, and the amount of drift of the output.

Overrange is any excess in the value of the measured variable above the upper range limit or below the lower range limit. When an instrument is subject to an overrange, it does not immediately return to operation within specifications when the overload is removed. A period of time called the *recovery time* is required to overcome the saturation effect of the overload. The *overrange limit* is the maximum overrange that can be applied to a measuring instrument without causing damage or permanent change in the performance of the device. Thus one reliability condition is that the measured variable not exceed the overrange limit.

Drift is an undesirable change over a specified period of time. *Zero drift* is a change in the output of the measuring instrument while the measured variable is held constant at its lower limit. *Sensitivity drift* is a change in the sensitivity of the instrument over the specified period. Zero drift raises or lowers the entire calibration curve of the instrument. Sensitivity drift changes the slope of the calibration curve. The reliability conditions specify an allowable amount of zero drift and sensitivity drift.

12.4 Static Characteristics

Static characteristics describe the accuracy of a measuring instrument at room conditions with the measured variable either constant or changing very slowly. *Accuracy* is the degree of conformity of the output of a measuring instrument to the ideal value of the measured variable as determined by some type of standard. Accuracy is measured by testing the measuring instrument with a specified procedure under specified conditions. The test is repeated a number of times, and the accuracy is given as the maximum positive and negative error (deviation from the ideal value). The *error* is defined as the difference between the measured value and the ideal value:

$$\text{Error} = \text{measured value} - \text{ideal value}$$

Accuracy is expressed in terms of the error in one of the following ways:

① In terms of the measured variable (e. g. , +1 ℃/−2 ℃);

② As a percentage of span (e. g. , ± 0.5% span);

③ As a percentage of actual output (e. g. , ± 1% of output).

The *repeatability* of a measuring instrument is a measure of the dispersion of the measurements (the standard deviation is another measure of dispersion). Accuracy and repeatability are not the same. Figure 12.1 uses the pattern of bullet holes in a target to illustrate the difference between repeatability and accuracy. Notice that a rifle, which is repeatable but not accurate, produces a tight pattern—but that the pattern is not centered on the bull's-eye. The distance from the center of the bull's-eye to the center of the pattern is called the *bias* or *systemic error*. A shooter who is aware of the bias may adjust accordingly and produce an accurate and repeatable pattern on the next try. An experienced operator will make a similar adjustment to compensate for bias in a controller. Thus an automatic controller that is repeatable but not accurate may still be very useful.

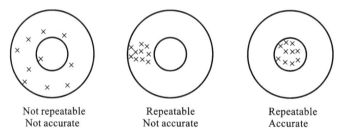

Fig. 12.1 Rifle target patterns illustrate the difference between repeatability and accuracy

Repeatability and reproducibility deal in slightly different ways with the degree of closeness among repeated measurements of the same value of the measured variable[4]. *Repeatability* is the maximum difference between several consecutive outputs for the same input when approached from the same direction in full-range traversals. *Reproducibility* is the maximum difference between a number of outputs for the same input, taken over an extended period of time, approaching from both directions. Reproducibility includes hysteresis, dead band, drift, and repeatability. The measurement of reproducibility must specify the time period used in the measurement. Reproducibility is obviously more difficult to determine because of the extended time period that is required.

The procedure of determining the accuracy of a measuring instrument is called *calibration*. It consists of three full-range traversals of the measuring instrument. The data from the calibration of a measuring instrument is presented in tabular form in a *calibration report*.

The measured accuracy and repeatability of the measuring instrument are taken directly from the calibration report. *Measured accuracy* is the maximum negative and positive errors in any of the readings in the calibration report. Repeatability is the greatest difference between the readings in the calibration report.

12.5 Velocity Measurement

12.5.1 Sensing Methods

Velocity is the rate of change of displacement or distance. It is measured in units of length per unit time. Velocity is a vector quantity that has both magnitude (speed) and direction. A change in velocity may constitute a change in speed, a change in direction, or both.

Angular velocity is the rate of change of angular displacement. It is measured in terms of radians per unit time or revolutions per unit time. Angular velocity measurement is more common in control systems than linear velocity measurement. When linear velocity is measured, it is often converted into an angular velocity and measured with an angular velocity transducer. Three methods of measuring angular velocity are considered in this section: DC tachometers, AC tachometers, and optical tachometers.

12.5.2 DC Tachometers

A DC *tachometer* is an electric generator used to measure angular velocity. The tachometer produces a DC voltage that is directly proportional to the angular velocity of the armature. Equation (12.4) defines the output voltage of the DC tachometer. The constant of proportionality is called the EMF constant, K_E, and it has units of volts per revolution per minute (V/rpm). The EMF constant depends on the physical parameters of the coil and the magnetic field.

$$E = K_E S = \frac{30 K_E \omega}{\pi} \tag{12.4}$$

where E = tachometer output, V;
K_E = EMF constant, V/rpm;
S = angular velocity, rpm;
ω = angular velocity, rad/s.

12.5.3 AC Tachometers

An AC tachometer is a three-phase electric generator with a three-phase rectifier on its output. The AC tachometer works well at high speeds, but the output becomes nonlinear at a low speed due to the voltage drop across the rectifiers (about 0.7V). For this reason, AC tachometers are usually limited to speed ranges of 100 to 1, compared with 1000 to 1 for DC tachometers. The AC tachometer has no brushes and has the same ability to withstand a contaminated environment as the brushless DC generator.

12.5.4 Optical Tachometers

An incremental encoder connected to a rotating shaft produces a sequence of pulses from which a digital velocity signal can be easily obtained. The major signal conditioning requirement is a timed counter. Equations (12.5) and (12.6) define the relationship between the shaft speed and the timed count for an optical tachometer.

$$S = \frac{60C}{NT_c} \quad (12.5)$$

$$C = \frac{SNT_c}{60} \quad (12.6)$$

where S = shaft speed, rpm;

N = number of pulses per shaft revolution;

C = total count during time interval T_c;

T_c = counter time interval, s.

Optical encoders can handle very large dynamic ranges with extremely high accuracy and excellent long-term stability.

New Words and Expressions

1. uncertainty *n.* 不确定度
2. fluid *adj.* 不固定的,易变的
3. confront with 使面临,使面对
4. observation *n.* 观测,(*pl*) 观察数据
5. dispersion *n.* 离差,分散
6. variability *n.* 可变性,变化性
7. lower range limit 范围下限
8. upper range limit 测量上限
9. span *n.* 跨度,范围
10. dead band 死区
11. increment *n.* 增量,增加
12. resolution *n.* 分辨率
13. threshold *n.* 阈值,门槛
14. probability *n.* 可能性,概率
15. over range 超量程
16. drift *n.* 漂移,漂流
17. specification *n.* 规格,说明书
18. calibration *n.* 标定,校准
19. accuracy *n.* 准确性,精确性
20. conformity *n.* 一致,符合
21. repeatability *n.* 重复性,再现性
22. bias *n.* 偏见,偏差
23. reproducibility *n.* 再现性,复现性
24. consecutive *adj.* 连续的,连贯的
25. traversal *n.* 遍历,横越
26. extended *adj.* 延伸的,长期的
27. tabular *adj.* 表格式的

28. velocity   *n.* 速度
29. radian   *n.* 弧度
30. revolution   *n.* 旋转，循环
31. tachometer   *n.* 转速计，转速表
32. withstand   *v.* 抵挡，禁得起
33. contaminate   *v.* 污染
34. incremental encoder   增量编码器
35. conditioning   *n.* 调节，调理

Notes

1. The mean gives us an estimate of the expected value of an observation, but it gives no idea of the dispersion or variability of the observations.
平均值给出了对观测数据期望值的估计，但不能指出观测数据的偏移或变化。

2. Operating characteristics include details about the measurement by, and operation of effects on the measuring instrument.
运行特性包括测量的细节以及影响测量仪器运行的因素。

3. Resolution, dead band, and sensitivity are different characteristics that relate in different ways to an increment of measurement.
relate to 涉及
分辨率、死区和灵敏度以不同的方法描述了测量增量不同的特性。

4. Repeatability and reproducibility deal in slightly different ways with the degree of closeness among repeated measurements of the same value of the measured variable.
deal with 论述，处理
重复性和再现性以细微不同的方法体现重复测量被测变量相同值的接近程度。

Exercises

I. Translate the phrases into English.

1. 不确定度   2. 观测数据   3. 采样   4. 算术平均   5. 期望值
6. 标准偏差   7. 下限   8. 上限   9. 跨度   10. 分辨率
11. 死区   12. 灵敏度   13. 阈值   14. 可靠性   15. 过量程
16. 恢复时间   17. 过载   18. 过量程极限   19. 漂移   20. 准确性
21. 误差   22. 重复性   23. 系统误差   24. 再现性   25. 校准
26. 线速度   27. 角速度   28. 弧度   29. 测速仪   30. 增量式编码器
31. 定时计数器   32. 稳定性

II. Answer the following questions according to the text.

1. What is the purpose of a measuring instrument?
2. How to define the span?
3. What is the other name for dead band?

4. How to distinguish sensitivity and gain?

5. What is overrange?

6. What does reproducibility include?

7. What is the definition of velocity?

8. How many methods do we have to measure angular velocity? What are they?

III. Translate the sentences into Chinese.

1. There is an uncertainty when we measure the value of a variable.

2. The sample mean is an estimate of the expected value of the next observation. The mean is computed by summing the observations and dividing by the number of observations.

3. The decision operation computes the error (desired value minus measured value) and use the error to form a control action.

4. The range consists of all values between the lower range limit and the upper range limit.

5. Accuracy is the degree of conformity of the output of a measuring instrument to the ideal value of the measured variable as determined by some type of standard.

6. Repeatability is the maximum difference between several consecutive outputs for the same input when approached from the same direction in full-range traversals.

7. Angular velocity is the rate of change of angular displacement.

8. An AC tachometer is a three-phase electric generator with a three-phase rectifier on its output.

Part 13

Switching Components

13.1 Introduction

A controller has two interfaces with the process it controls: one is the input to the controller, the other is the output from the controller. Sensors and signal conditioners handle the input side. Various types of switching elements, actuators, control valves, heaters, and electric motors handle the output side.

Switches are devices that make or break the connection in an electric circuit. The switching action may be accomplished mechanically by an actuator, electromechanically by a solenoid, or electronically by a solid-state device. All these three methods of accomplishing the switching action are used in control systems. Switches turn on electric motors and heating elements, sense the presence of an object, regulate the speed of an electric motor, actuate solenoid valves that control pneumatic or hydraulic cylinders, and initiate actions in sequential control systems.

The purpose of this part is to discuss, select and specify switching components.

13.2 Mechanical Switching Components

Mechanical switching components are used in the manipulating element of some process control systems. They are often used in sequential control systems to perform a set of operations in a prescribed manner.

13.2.1 Mechanical Switches

Mechanical *switches* use one or more pairs of contacts to make or break an electric circuit. The contacts may be normally open (NO) or normally closed (NC). A normally open switch will close the circuit path between the two terminals when the switch is actuated and will open the circuit path when the switch is deactuated[1]. A normally closed switch will open the circuit path when the switch is actuated and will close the circuit path when the switch is deactuated. The more common actuating mechanisms include pushbuttons, toggles, lever plungers, and rotary knobs.

The switching action may be momentary-action or maintained-action. In a *momentary-action* switch, the operator pushes the button, moves the toggle, or rotates the knob to change the position of the contacts. When the operator releases the switch, the contacts return to the normal position. When an operator actuates a *maintained-action* switch, the contacts remain in the new position after the operator releases the actuator[2]. In most momentary-action switches, the actuator returns to its original position when released, and in most maintained-action switches, the actuator remains in the new position when released. However, in some maintained-action switches the actuator returns to the original position, even though the contacts remain in the new position.

Mechanically actuated switches may be operated manually by an operator or automatically by fluid pressure, liquid level, temperature, flow, thermal overload, a cam, or the presence of an object. Figure 13.1 shows standard wiring diagram symbols for various types of switches. The limit switches in Fig. 13.1 are actuated by a cam or some other object that engages the switch actuator. Pressure-actuated switches open or close their contacts at a given pressure. Liquid level-actuated switches open or close their contacts at a given liquid level. Temperature-actuated switches open or close their contacts at a given temperature. Flow-actuated switches open or close their contacts when a given flow rate is sensed. The overload switches are circuit breakers that open a normally closed contact when an overload condition occurs. Overload switches are intended to protect motors and other equipment from damage caused by an overload condition.

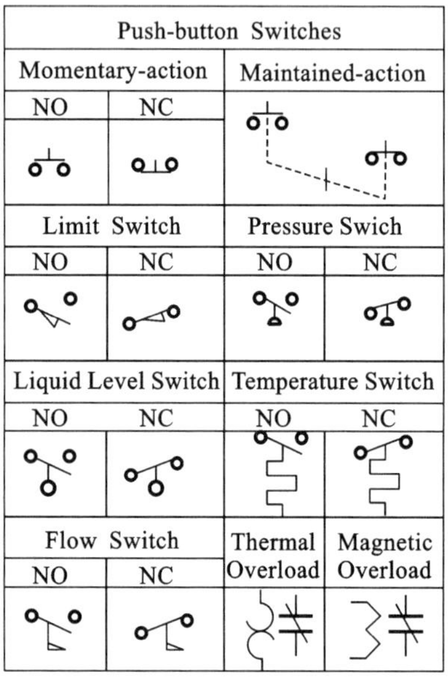

Fig. 13.1 Wiring diagram symbols for mechanical switches

13.2.2 Relays

A *relay* is a set of switches that are actuated when electric current passes through a coil of wire. The electric current passing through the coil of wire generates a magnetic field about the core of the coil. This magnetic field pulls a movable arm that forces the contact to open or close. The *pull-in current* is the minimum coil current that causes the arm to move from its OFF position to its ON position. The *drop-out current* is the maximum coil current that will allow the arm to move from its ON position to its OFF position. Figure 13.2 illustrates two *control relays*, one with two switches, the other with four switches. The relay coils are represented schematically by the circles with the designation 1CR and 3CR. The CR signifies a control relay, and the numbers 1 and 3 are used to distinguish between the two control relays. Each relay in a drawing must have a unique designation.

The relay is actuated (or energized) by completing the circuit branch that contains the

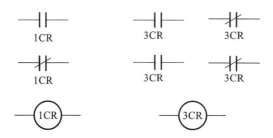

Fig. 13.2 Control relays using the coil designation (e. g., 1CR, 3CR) to identify the contacts that actuated by the coil

relay coil[3]. The relay coil designation is used to identify the contacts that are actuated by a particular relay coil. Normally open contacts are designated by a pair of parallel lines. Normally closed contacts are designated by a pair of parallel lines with a diagonal line connecting the two parallel lines. A normally open contact will close the circuit path when the relay coil is energized and will open the circuit path when the relay is deenergized. A normally closed contact will open the circuit path when the relay coil is energized and will close the circuit path when the relay coil is deenergized.

Notice that relay 1CR has one normally open contact and one normally closed contact. Relay 3CR has two normally open contacts and two normally closed contacts. This method of using the relay coil designation to identify the relay contacts is necessary because the contacts may occur anywhere in an electric circuit diagram. The designation identifies which relay coil actuates each set of contacts.

13.2.3 Time-Delay Relays

Time-delay relays are control relays that have provisions for a delayed switching action (see Fig. 13.3). The delay in switching is usually adjustable, and it may take place when the coil is energized or when the coil is deenergized. An arrow is used to identify the switching direction in which the time delay takes place. In relay 1TR, the delay occurs when the coil is energized. Contact 1TR delays before it closes. When coil 1TR is deenergized, contact 1TR opens immediately. In relay 2TR, the delay also occurs when the coil is energized. The 2TR contact delays before it opens and closes immediately when the coil is deenergized. In relays 3TR and 4TR, the delay occurs when the coil is deenergized. Contact 3TR closes immediately when coil 3TR is energized and delays before it opens when the coil is deenergized. Contact 4TR opens immediately when coil 4TR is energized, and delays before it closes when coil 4TR is deenergized.

In a time-delay relay, the delay occurs in the direction in which the arrow is pointing.

13.2.4 Contactors and Motor Starters

Relays with heavy-duty contacts are used to switch circuits that use large amounts of electric power. When the circuit load is an electric motor, the relay is called a *motor starter*; otherwise, it is called a *contactor*. An example of a relay for switching a three-

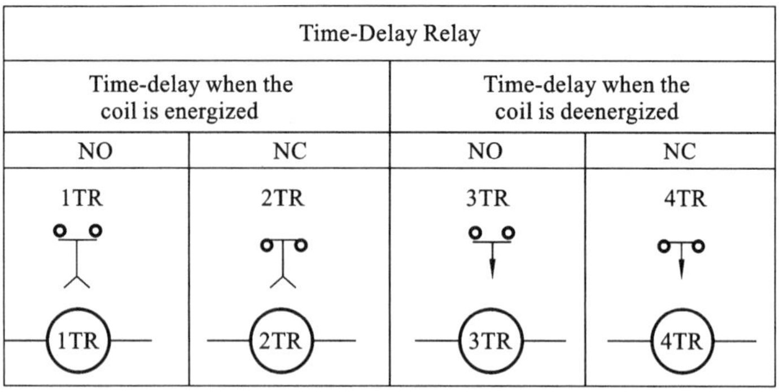

Time-Delay Relay			
Time-delay when the coil is energized		Time-delay when the coil is deenergized	
NO	NC	NO	NC
1TR	2TR	3TR	4TR

Fig. 13.3 In time-delay relays, the arrow points in the direction in which the delayed action occurs

phase system is shown in Fig. 13.4. The three heavy contacts are used to switch the three lines supplying electric power to the load. The two light contacts are used in the control circuit.

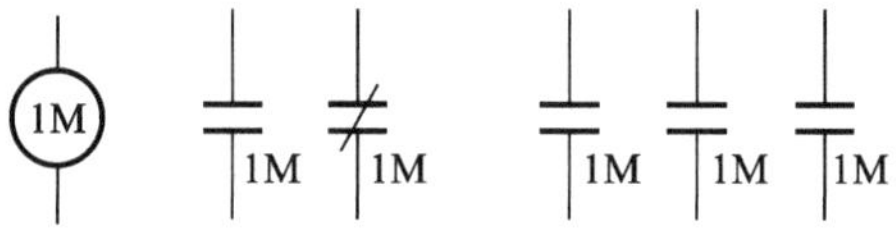

Fig. 13.4 Motor starters and contactors have three large contactors that are used to switch large amounts of electric power. The small auxiliary contacts are used in the control circuit

Figure 13.5 illustrates a circuit for starting and stopping a 480-V AC three-phase electric motor. The two momentary-action push-button switches in the 115-V AC circuit are the start-stop station for the motor. When the START button is pressed, coil 1M is energized, closing all four 1M contacts. The three large contacts connect the three 480-V AC lines to the motor. The small contact in parallel with the START switch is used to hold the circuit closed after the START button is released. The small contact is called a "holding contact" because it "holds" coil 1M in the energized condition after the operator releases the START button[4]. When the operator presses the STOP button, the circuit breaks and all four 1M contacts open. The circuit remains deenergized after the STOP button is released because the 1M holding contact is open.

13.3 Solid-State Components

Solid-state components are used in a variety of ways in control systems. For example, they are used to convert a DC voltage into a controlled AC voltage, vary the AC power delivered to a load. They are used as ON/OFF switches to control motors, solenoid

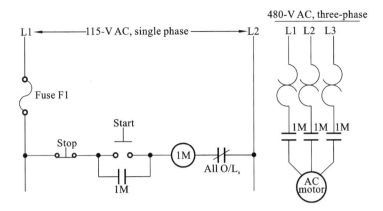

Fig. 13.5 Control circuit for starting a large AC motor

valves, and a light. They are also used as electronic switches in a brushless DC motor. They are used in a full-wave bridge rectifier to control large DC motors, in DC power amplifiers to control DC servo motors, used in a phase discriminator to control the thickness of a sheet, and used in a three-phase converter and inverter to control the speed of a large AC motor.

The purpose of this section is to describe the names, symbols, and operation of the solid-state components most frequently used in control.

13.3.1 Diodes

Diodes are used as rectifiers in DC power supplies and as one-way "valves" to block or bypass undesired electric currents. The voltampere characteristic of the diode is shown in Fig. 13.6. The diode has three operating regions depending on the anode-to-cathode voltage (u). If the anode-to-cathode voltage is positive, the diode is said to be forward biased; if the voltage is negative, the diode is reverse biased. In operating region 1, the diode is forward biased and conducts electric current with very low resistance. In region 2, the diode is reversed biased and blocks electric current with high resistance. In region 3, the reverse bias has increased to the point of breakdown and the diode conducts electric current. For most applications, operation in region 3 is avoided. An exception to this rule is the zener diode, which is operated in region 3 as a voltage regulator.

13.3.2 Transistors

Transistors are used in control systems as switches, amplifiers, and oscillators. There are two types of transistors, the NPN type and the PNP type. The operating characteristics of NPN and PNP transistors are the same except that the directions of the voltages and currents are opposite. The following discussion is confined to the NPN transistor.

An NPN transistor has three terminals called the collector, base, and emitter, as shown in Fig. 13.7. Transistors are essentially controlled-current amplifiers. A relatively

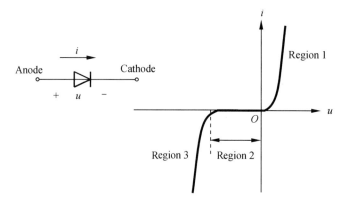

Fig. 13.6　Voltampere characteristic of the diode

small current entering the base is used to control a much larger current entering through the collector. Both currents leave through the emitter. The ratio of the collector current (i_c) to the base current (i_b) is called the β (beta) of the transistor ($\beta = i_c/i_b$). The β of a transistor ranges from 20 to 200, and it varies from one transistor to another, even if they are of the same type. Aging and changes in temperature may also cause the β to change.

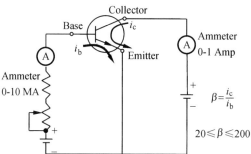

Fig. 13.7　Test circuit for an NPN transistor

A transistor may be used in one of three different amplifier configurations, depending on which terminal is common to the input and the output. The three configurations are common-base, common-emitter, and common-collector. The common-emitter and common-collector amplifiers may be combined to form multi-stage amplifiers with increased voltage and current gains.

13.3.3　Silicon-Controlled Rectifiers

One of the major uses of solid-states components is in switching circuits of all sizes. Although transistors are used in some switching circuits, power switching is the domain of the *silicon-controlled rectifier* (SCR) and the triac. The SCR is a latching switch—the SCR can be turned ON by a short pulse of control current into the gate and it remains ON as long as current is flowing from the anode to the cathode. Its characteristics will be discussed in the following part.

13.3.4 Triacs

The *triac* was developed as a means of providing improved controls for AC power[5]. The major difference between the triac and the SCR is that the triac can conduct in both directions, whereas the SCR can conduct in only one direction. A typical triac circuit is shown in Fig. 13.8. A positive or negative gate current of sufficient amplitude will trigger the triac ON when u_{21} is either positive or negative. The first triggering pulse turns the triac on during the positive half-cycle. The triac remains on until the AC voltage reverses and turns the triac OFF. The next triggering pulse turns the triac on during the negative half-cycle. The triac again remains ON until the AC voltage reverses and turns the triac OFF. The trigger circuit determines when the triggering pulse will turn the triac ON. This in turn determines how much current is delivered to the load.

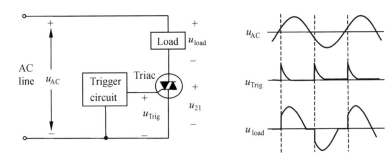

Fig. 13.8 Basic triac circuit for control of an AC load

🔍 New Words and Expressions

1. interface   *n.* 接口, 界面
2. conditioner   *n.* 调节器
3. switch   *n.* 开关
4. actuator   *n.* 执行器, 驱动器
5. valve   *n.* 阀, 气门
6. electromechanical   *adj.* 机电的
7. solenoid   *n.* 电磁线圈
8. actuate   *v.* 驱使, 激励
9. pneumatic   *adj.* 气动的, 可充气的
10. hydraulic   *adj.* 液压的, 水力的
11. cylinder   *n.* 圆筒, 汽缸
12. initiate   *v.* 开始, 发起
13. sequential   *adj.* 连续的
14. prescribe   *v.* 规定
15. contact   *n.* 触点, 接触
16. toggle   *n.* 拴扣
17. lever   *n.* 杠杆, 手柄
18. knob   *n.* 旋钮, 按钮
19. momentary   *adj.* 瞬间的, 短暂的
20. cam   *n.* 凸轮
21. circuit breaker   断路器
22. relay   *n.* 继电器
23. pull-in   *n.* 接通
24. drop-out current   开断电流
25. signify   *v.* 表示, 意味
26. energize   *v.* 激励, 供给……能量
27. diagonal   *adj.* 对角线的, 斜的
28. provision   *n.* 准备, 规定

29. heavy-duty   *adj.* 耐用的,重型的
30. holding   *n.* 保持,自动封锁
31. solid-state   *adj.* 固态的
32. rectifier   *n.* 整流器
33. discriminator   *n.* 鉴相器,鉴别器
34. converter   *n.* 转换器,变换器
35. zener diode   稳压二极管
36. triac   *n.* 双向晶闸管,三端双向可控硅开关元件

Notes

1. A normally open switch will close the circuit path between the two terminals when the switch is actuated and will open the circuit path when the switch is deactuated.

当驱动开关时,常开开关会闭合两个终端之间的电路通道;当撤除驱动后,开关会断开电路通道。

2. When an operator actuates a maintained-action switch, the contacts remain in the new position after the operator releases the actuator.

操作者驱动一个持续动作的开关,当撤除驱动后,触点仍然维持在新的位置。

3. The relay is actuated (or energized) by completing the circuit branch that contains the relay coil.

complete   把(电路)接通

通过接通继电器线圈所在的分支电路打开继电器。

4. The small contact is called a "holding contact" because it "holds" coil 1M in the energized condition after the operator releases the START button.

小的触点为"自锁触点",因为在操作者释放"开始"按钮后,这个触点能将线圈 1M"自锁"在通电状态。

5. The triac was developed as a means of providing improved controls for AC power.

双向可控硅已作为对交流电网进行改进控制的工具。

Exercises

I. Translate the phrases into English.

1. 接口
2. 调节器
3. 开关
4. 驱动器(执行器)
5. 电磁阀
6. 连续控制系统
7. 触点
8. 常开
9. 常闭
10. 限位开关
11. 继电器
12. 延时继电器
13. 接通(吸合)电流
14. 开断(释放)电流
15. 电机起动器
16. 接触器
17. 自锁触点
18. 整流器
19. 变流器
20. 逆变器
21. 二极管
22. 阳极
23. 阴极
24. 正向偏置
25. 反向偏置
26. 阻断
27. 稳压二极管
28. 晶体管

29. 集电极 30. 基极 31. 发射极 32. 共发射极
33. 双向晶闸管 34. 正半周 35. 触发电流

II. Answer the following questions according to the text.

1. What are switches?
2. What do mechanical switches use to make or break an electric circuit?
3. What is a relay?
4. Which kind of contacts does a pair of parallel lines designate?
5. When the circuit load is an electric motor, what is the relay called? Otherwise what is it called?
6. What effects do diodes have?
7. If the anode-to-cathode voltage is positive, how is the diode?
8. What are transistors used as in control systems?
9. What is the major difference between the triac and the SCR?

III. Translate the sentences into Chinese.

1. A controller has two interfaces with the process it controls: one is the input to the controller, the other is the output from the controller.
2. Normally closed contacts are designated by parallel lines with a diagonal line connecting the two parallel lines.
3. In a time-delay relay, the delay occurs in the direction in which the arrow is pointing.
4. A normally closed contact will open the circuit path when the relay coil is energized and will close the circuit path when the relay coil is deenergized.
5. The three heavy contacts are used to switch the three lines supplying electric power to the load. The two light contacts are used in the control circuit.
6. The SCR can be turned ON by a short pulse of control current into the gate and it remains ON as long as current is flowing from the anode to the cathode.

Part 14

Power Semiconductor Switches

14.1 Introduction

The increased power capabilities, ease of control, and reduced costs of modern power semiconductor devices compared to those of just a few years ago have made converters affordable in a large number of applications. In order to clearly understand the feasibility of these new topologies and applications, it is essential that the characteristics of available power devices be put in perspective. To do this, a brief summary of the terminal characteristics and the voltage, current, and switching speed capabilities of currently available power devices are presented in this part.

If the power semiconductor devices can be considered as ideal switches, the analysis of converter topologies becomes much easier. This approach has the advantage that the details of devices operation will not obscure the basic operation of the circuit. Therefore, the important converter characteristics can be more clearly understood. The summary of device characteristics will enable us to determine how much the device characteristics can be idealized.

Presently available power semiconductor devices can be classified into three groups according to their degree of controllability:

① *Diodes*. On and off states controlled by the power circuit;

② *Thyristors*. Latched on by a control signal but must be turned off by the power circuit[1];

③ *Controllable switches*. Turned on and off by control signals.

The controlled switch category includes several device types including bipolar junction transistors (BJTs), metals-oxide-semiconductor field effect transistors (MOSFETs), gate turn off (GTO) thyristors, and insulated gate bipolar transistors (IGBTs). There have been major advances in recent years in this category of devices.

14.2 Thyristors

The SCR is also called as the thyristor. The circuit symbol for the thyristor and its i-u characteristics are shown in Fig. 14.1(a) and Fig. 14.1(b). The main current flows from the anode (A) to the cathode (K). In its off-state, the thyristor can block a forward polarity voltage and not conduct, as is shown in Fig. 14.1(b) by the off-state portion of the i-u characteristics.

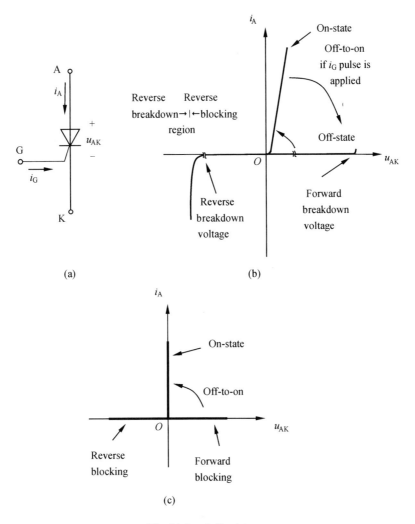

Fig. 14.1 A thyristor

(a) Symbol (b) i-u characteristics (c) Idealized characteristics

The thyristor can be triggered into the on state by applying a pulse of positive gate current for a short duration provided that the device is in its forward-blocking state. The resulting i-u relationship is shown by the on-state portion of the characteristic shown in Fig. 14.1(b). The forward voltage drop in the on state is only a few volts (typically 1-3V depending on the device blocking voltage rating).

Once the device begins to conduct, it is latched on and the gate current can be removed[2]. The thyristor cannot be turned off by the gate, and the thyristor conducts as a diode. Only when the anode current tries to go negative, under the influence of the circuit in which the thyristor is connected, does the thyristor turn off and the current go to zero. This allows the gate to regain control in order to turn the device on at some controllable time after it has again entered the forward-blocking state.

In reverse bias at voltages below the reverse breakdown voltage, only a negligibly small leakage current flows in the thyristor, as shown in Fig. 14.1(b). Usually the thyristor voltage ratings for forward- and reverse-blocking voltages are the same. The thyristor current ratings are specified in terms of maximum rms and average currents that it is capable of conducting.

Using the same arguments as for diodes, the thyristor can be represented by the idealized characteristics shown in Fig. 14.1(c) in analyzing converter topologies.

Depending on the application requirements, various types of thyristors are available. In addition to voltage and current ratings, turn-off time t_q, and the forward voltage drop, other characteristics that must be considered include the rate of rise of the current (di/dt) at turn-on and the rate of rise of voltage (du/dt) at turn-off.

14.3 Metal-Oxide-Semiconductor Field Effect Transistors

The circuit symbol of an *n*-channel MOSFET is shown in Fig. 14.2(a). It is a voltage-controlled device, as is indicated by the *i-u* characteristics shown in Fig. 14.2(b). The device is fully on and approximates a closed switch when the gate-source voltage is above the threshold value, $U_{GS(th)}$. The idealized characteristics of the device operating as a switch are shown in Fig. 14.2(c).

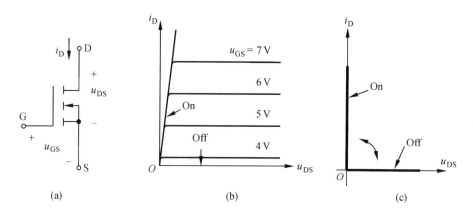

Fig. 14.2 An *n*-channel MOSFET

(a) Symbol (b) *i-u* characteristics (c) Idealized characteristics

Metal-oxide-semiconductor field effect transistors require the continuous application of a gate-source voltage of appropriate magnitude in order to be in the on state. No gate current flows except during the transitions from on to off or vice versa when the gate capacitance is being charged or discharged. The switching times are very short, being in the range of a few tens of nanoseconds to a few hundred nanoseconds depending on the device type.

The on-state resistance $r_{DS(on)}$ of the MOSFET between the drain and source increases rapidly with the device blocking voltage rating. Only devices with small voltage ratings, which have low on-state resistance and hence small conduction losses, are available.

However, because of their fast switching speed, the switching losses can be small. From a total power loss standpoint, 300-400V MOSFETs compete with the bipolar transistor only if the switching frequency is in excess of 30-100 kHz. However, no definite statement can be made about the crossover frequency because it depends on the operating voltages, with low voltages favoring the MOSFET.

Metal-oxide-semiconductor field effect transistors are available in voltage ratings in excess of 1000V but with small current ratings with up to 100A at small voltage ratings. The maximum gate-source voltage is ±20V, although MOSFETs that can be controlled by 5V signals are available.

Because their on-state resistance has a positive temperature coefficient, MOSFETs are easily paralleled. This causes the device conducting the higher current to heat up and thus forces it to equitably share its current with the other MOSFETs in parallel.

14.4 Gate Turn-Off Thyristors

The circuit symbol for the GTO is shown in Fig. 14.3(a) and its steady-state i-u characteristics are shown in Fig. 14.3(b).

Like the thyristor, the GTO can be turned on by a short-duration gate current pulse, and once in the on-state, the GTO may stay on without any further gate current. However, unlike the thyristor, the GTO can be turned off by applying a negative gate-cathode voltage, therefore causing a sufficiently large negative gate current to flow. This negative gate current needs only to flow for a few microseconds (during the turn-off time), but it must have a very large magnitude, typically as large as one-third the anode current being turned off. The GTOs can block negative voltages whose magnitude depends on the details of the GTO design. Idealized characteristics of the device operating as a switch are shown in Fig. 14.3(c).

Even though the GTO is a controllable switch in the same category as MOSFETs and BJTs, its turn-off switching transient is different from that of MOSFETs. This is because presently available GTOs cannot be used for inductive turn-off unless a snubber circuit is connected across the GTO [see Fig. 14.4(a)]. This is a consequence of the fact that a large du/dt that accompanies inductive turn-off cannot be tolerated by present-day GTOs. Therefore a circuit to reduce du/dt at turn-off that consists of R, C and D, as shown in

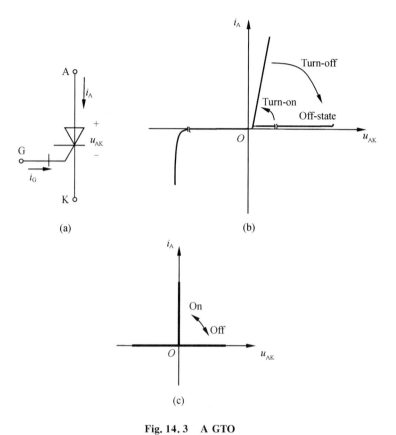

Fig. 14.3 A GTO

(a) Symbol   (b) i-u characteristics   (c) Idealized characteristics

Fig. 14.4 (a), must be used across the GTO. The resulting waveforms are shown in Fig. 14.4(b), where du/dt is significantly reduced compared to the du/dt that would result without the turn-off snubber circuit.

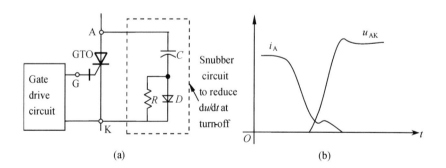

Fig. 14.4 Gate turn-off transient characteristics

(a) Snubber circuit   (b) GTO turn-off characteristics

The on-state voltage (2-3V) of a GTO is slightly higher than those of thyristors. The GTO switching speeds are in the range of a few microseconds to $25\mu s$. Because of their capability to handle large voltages (up to 4.5kV) and large currents (up to a few kiloamperes), the GTO is used when a switch is needed for high voltages and large currents in a switching frequency range of a few hundred hertz to 10kHz.

14.5 Insulated Gate Bipolar Transistors

The circuit symbol for an IGBT is shown in Fig. 14.5(a) and its i-u characteristics are shown in Fig. 14.5(b). The IGBTs have some of the advantages of the MOSFET, the BJT, and the GTO combined. Similar to the MOSFET, the IGBT has a high impedance gate, which requires only a small amount of energy to switch the device. Like the BJT, the IGBT has a small on-state voltage even in devices with large blocking voltage ratings (for example, U_{on} is 2-3V in a 1000V device). Similar to the GTO, IGBTs can be designed to block negative voltage.

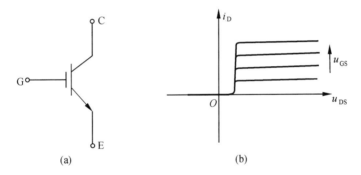

Fig. 14.5 An IGBT

(a) Symbol (b) i-u characteristics

Insulated gate bipolar transistors have turn-on and turn-off times on the order of $1\mu s$ and are available in module ratings as large as 1700V and 1200A. Voltage ratings of up to 2-3kV are projected.

14.6 Desired Characteristics in Controllable Switches

As mentioned in the introduction, several types of semiconductor power devices including BJTs, MOSFETs, GTOs, and IGBTs can be turned on and off by control signals applied to the control terminal of the device. These devices we term controllable switches are represented in a generic manner by the circuit symbol shown in Fig. 14.6. No current flows when the switch is off, and when it is on, current can flow in the direction of the arrow only. The ideal controllable switch has the following characteristics:

① Block arbitrarily large forward and reverse voltages with zero current flow

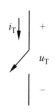

Fig. 14.6 Generic controllable switch

when off;

② Conduct arbitrarily large currents with zero voltage drop when on;

③ Switch from on to off or vice versa instantaneously when triggered;

④ Vanishingly small power required from control source to trigger the switch.

Real devices, as we intuitively expect, do not have these ideal characteristics and hence will dissipate power when they are used in the numerous applications already mentioned. If they dissipate too much power, the devices can fail and, in doing so, not only will destroy themselves but also may damage the other system components.

The following characteristics in a controllable switch are desirable:

① Small leakage current in the off state.

② Small on-state voltage U_{on} to minimize on-state power losses.

③ Short turn-on and turn-off time. This will permit the device to be used at high switching frequencies.

④ Large forward- and reverse-voltage-blocking capability. This will minimize the need for series connection of several devices, which complicates the control and protection of the switches. Moreover, most of the device types have a minimum on-state voltage regardless of their blocking voltage rating. A series connection of several such devices would lead to a higher total on-state voltage and hence higher conduction losses. In most (but not all) converter circuits, a diode is placed across the controllable switch to allow the current to flow in the reverse direction. In those circuits, controllable switches are not required to have any significant reverse-voltage-blocking capability.

⑤ High on-state current rating. In high-current applications, this would minimize the need to connect several devices in parallel, thereby avoiding the problem of current sharing.

⑥ Positive temperature coefficient of on-state resistance. This ensures that paralleled devices will share the total current equally.

⑦ Small control power required to switch the device. This will simplify the control circuit design.

⑧ Capability to withstand rated voltage and rated current simultaneously while switching. This will eliminate the need for external protection (snubber) circuits across the device.

⑨ Large du/dt and di/dt ratings. This will minimize the need for external circuits otherwise needed to limit du/dt and di/dt in the device so that it is not damaged.

New Words and Expressions

1. feasibility　　*n.* 可行性,可能性
2. in perspective　　正确地(看待)
3. currently　　*adv.* 当前,一般地
4. obscure　　*v.* 使难理解
5. latch　　*v.* 闭锁,闩上
6. regain　　*v.* 恢复
7. channel　　*n.* 沟道
8. coefficient　　*n.* 系数
9. equitably　　*adv.* 公正地
10. transient　　*n.* 瞬态,瞬变现象
11. snubber　　*n.* 缓冲器
12. generic　　*adj.* 一般的
13. arbitrarily　　*adv.* 任意地
14. vanishingly　　*adv.* 趋于零地
15. intuitively　　*adv.* 直觉地,直观地
16. regardless of　　不管,不顾

Notes

1. Latched on by a control signal but must be turned off by the power circuit.
由控制信号(控制器件)导通,但必须通过主电路才能使其断开。

2. Once the device begins to conduct, it is latched on and the gate current can be removed.
一旦器件开始导通,它就自锁(门极失去作用),就可以移去门极电流。

Exercises

I. Translate the phrases into English.

1. 功率容量　　2. 功率器件　　3. 晶闸管　　4. 导通
5. 正向阻断　　6. 通态　　7. 关断状态　　8. 反向击穿电压
9. 漏电流　　10. 电流额定值　　11. 漏极　　12. 门极
13. 缓冲电路　　14. 均流　　15. 额定电压　　16. 可控开关

II. Answer the following questions according to the text.

1. What are the advantages of modern power semiconductor devices?
2. When can the thyristor be triggered into the on state?
3. When does the thyristor turn off and the current go to zero?
4. What is MOSFET?
5. How can the GTO be turned off?
6. Why is a diode placed across the controllable switch in most converter circuits?
7. What is IGBT?

III. Translate the sentences into Chinese.

1. In its off-state, the thyristor can block a forward polarity voltage and not conduct.

2. The device is fully on and approximates a closed switch when the gate-source voltage is above the threshold value, $U_{GS(th)}$.

3. The GTOs can block negative voltages whose magnitude depends on the details of the GTO design.

4. Because of their capability to handle large voltages (up to 4.5kV) and large currents (up to a few kiloamperes), the GTO is used when a switch is needed for high voltages and large currents in a switching frequency range of a few hundred hertz to 10kHz.

Part 15

Rectifiers and Inverters

15.1 Introduction

In some applications, such as battery chargers and a class of DC- and AC-motor drives, it is necessary for the DC voltage to be controllable. The AC to controlled-DC conversion is accomplished in line-frequency phase-controlled converts by means of thyristors. In the past, these converters were used in a large number of applications for controlling the flow of electric power. Owing to the increasing availability of better controllable switches in high voltage and current ratings, new use of these thyristor converters nowadays is primarily in three-phase, high-power applications. This is particularly true in applications, most of them at high power levels, where it is necessary or desirable to be able to control the power flow in both directions between the AC and the DC sides. Examples of such applications are converters in high-voltage DC power transmission and some DC motor and AC motor drives with regenerative capabilities.

As the name of these converters implies, the line-frequency voltages are present on their AC side. In these converters, the instant at which a thyristor begins or ceases to conduct depends on the line-frequency AC voltage waveforms and the control inputs. Moreover, the transfer or commutation of current from one device to the next occurs naturally because of the presence of these AC voltages.

It should be noted that the uncontrollable, line-frequency diode rectifiers are a subset of the controlled converters.

A fully controlled converter is shown in Fig. 15.1(a) in block diagram form. For given AC line voltages, the *average* DC-side voltage can be controlled from a positive maximum to a negative minimum value in a continuous manner. The converter DC current I_d (or i_d on an instantaneous basis) cannot change direction, as will be explained later. Therefore, a converter of this type can operate in only two quadrants (of the U_d-I_d plane), as shown in Fig. 15.1(b). Here, the positive values of U_d and I_d imply *rectification* where the power flow is from the AC to the DC side. In an *inverter* mode, U_d becomes negative (but I_d stays positive) and the power is transferred from the DC to the AC side. The inverter mode of operation on a sustained basis is possible only if a source of power, such as batteries, is present on the DC side.

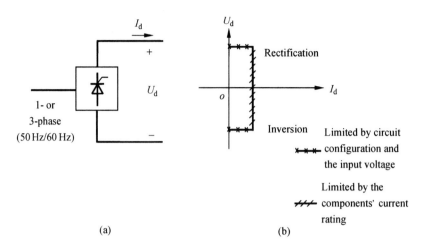

Fig. 15.1 Line-frequency controlled converter

In some applications, such as in reversible-speed DC motor drives with regenerative braking, the converter must be capable of operating in all four quadrants. This is accomplished by connecting two two-quadrant converters (described above) in antiparallel or back to back.

In analyzing the converters in this part, the thyristors are assumed to be ideal, except for the consideration of the thyristor turn-off time t_q.

15.2 Basic Rectifier Concepts

Rectification of AC voltages and currents is accomplished by means of diodes. Several simple circuits are considered to illustrate the basic concepts.

15.2.1 Pure Resistive Load

Consider the circuit of Fig. 15.2(a), with a sinusoidal voltage source u_s. The waveforms in Fig. 15.2(b) show that both the load voltage u_d and the current i_d have an average (DC) component. Because of the large ripple in u_d and i_d, this circuit is of little practical significance[1].

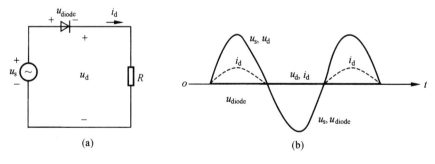

Fig. 15.2 Basic rectifier with a load resistance

15.2.2 Inductance Load

Let us consider the load to be inductive, with an inductor in series with a resistor, as shown in Fig. 15.3(a). Prior to $t=0$, the voltage u_s is negative and the current in the circuit is zero. Subsequent to $t=0$, the diode becomes forward biased and a current begins to flow. Then, the diode can be replaced by a short one, as shown in the equivalent circuit of Fig. 15.3(e). The current in this circuit is governed by the following differential equation:

$$u_s = Ri_d + L\frac{di_d}{dt} \tag{15.1}$$

where the voltage across the inductor $u_L = Ldi_d/dt$. The resulting voltages and current are shown in Figs. 15.3(b) and (c). Until t_1, $u_s > u_R$ (hence $u_L = u_s - u_R$ is positive), the current builds up, and the inductor stored energy increases. Beyond t_1, u_L becomes negative, and the current begins to decrease. After t_2, the input voltage u_s becomes negative but the current is still positive and the diode must conduct because of the inductor stored energy.

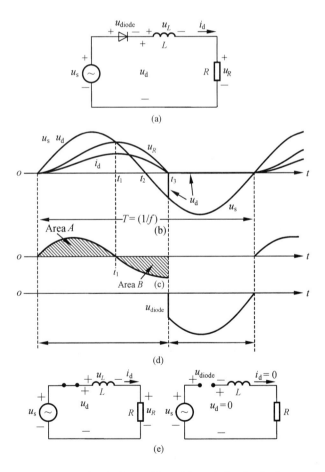

Fig. 15.3 Basic rectifier with an inductive load

The instant t_3, when the current goes to zero and the diode stops conducting, can be obtained as follows: the inductor equation $u_L = L\mathrm{d}i_d/\mathrm{d}t$ can be rearranged as

$$\frac{1}{L}u_L \mathrm{d}t = \mathrm{d}i_\mathrm{d} \tag{15.2}$$

Integrating both sides of the above equation between zero and t_3 and recognizing that $i_\mathrm{d}(0)$ and $i_\mathrm{d}(t_3)$ are both zero give

$$\frac{1}{L}\int_0^{t_3} u_L \mathrm{d}t = \int_{i(0)}^{i(t_3)} \mathrm{d}i_\mathrm{d} = i_\mathrm{d}(t_3) - i_\mathrm{d}(0) = 0 \tag{15.3}$$

From the above equation, we can observe that

$$\int_0^{t_3} u_L \mathrm{d}t = 0 \tag{15.4}$$

A graphical interpretation of the above equation is as follows: Equation (15.4) can be written as

$$\int_0^{t_1} u_L \mathrm{d}t + \int_{t_1}^{t_3} u_L \mathrm{d}t = 0 \tag{15.5}$$

which in terms of the volt-second Area A and Area B of Fig. 15.3(c) is

$$\text{Area } A - \text{Area } B = 0 \tag{15.6}$$

Therefore, the current goes to zero at t_3 when Area $A = $ Area B in Fig. 15.3(c).

Beyond t_3, the voltages across both R and L are zero and a reverse polarity voltage ($= -u_s$) appears across the diode, as shown in Fig. 15.3(d). These waveforms repeat with the time period $T = 1/f$.

The load voltage u_d becomes negative during the interval from t_2 to t_3. Therefore comparison to the case of purely resistive load of Fig. 15.2(a), the average load voltage is lower.

15.2.3 Load with an Internal DC Voltage

Next, we will consider the circuit of Fig. 15.4(a) where the load consists of an inductor L and a DC voltage E_d. The diode begins to conduct at t_1 when u_s exceeds E_d. The current reaches its peak at t_2 (when u_s is again equal to E_d) and decays to zero at t_3, with t_3 determined by the requirement that the volt-second area A be equal to area B in the plot of u_L shown in Fig. 15.4(c). The voltage across the diode is shown in Fig. 15.4(d).

15.3 Practical Thyristor Converters

The circuit of a practical thyristor converter is drawn in Fig. 15.5(a), where the load is represented by a DC voltage source E_d in series with L_d, which may be a part of the load; otherwise it is externally added. A small resistance r_d is also included. Such a representation applies to battery chargers and DC motor drives. The waveforms are shown in Fig. 15.5(b) for $\alpha = 45°$ and a continuously flowing i_d. There is a finite commutation interval γ due to L_s^2. Also due to L_s and the ripple in i_d, the u_d waveform differs from the

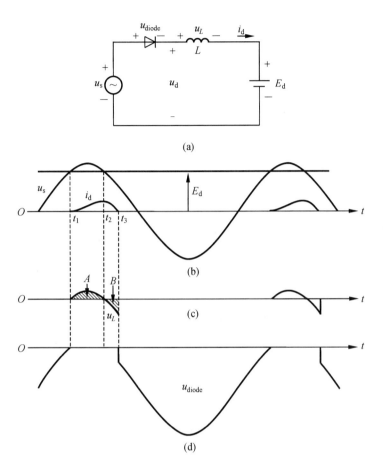

Fig. 15.4 Basic rectifier with an internal DC voltage

instantaneous $|u_s(t)|$ waveform by the voltage drop across L_s^3. It is reasonable to express the average value of u_d in terms of the equation $U_d = 0.9 U_s \cos \alpha - \frac{2}{\pi}\omega L_s I_d$, if i_d is flowing continuously:

$$U_d \approx 0.9 U_s \cos \alpha - \frac{2}{\pi}\omega L_s I_{d,\min} \tag{15.7}$$

where $I_{d,\min}$ is the minimum value of i_d that occurs at $\omega t \approx \alpha$.

To obtain the average value I_d of the DC current in the circuit of Fig. 15.5(a),

$$u_d = r_d i_d + L_d \frac{di_d}{dt} + E_d \tag{15.8}$$

Integrating both sides of Eq. (15.8) over one time period T and dividing by T, we get the average voltages:

$$\frac{1}{T}\int_0^T u_d\,dt = \frac{r_d}{T}\int_0^T i_d\,dt + \frac{L_d}{T}\int_{I_d(0)}^{I_d(T)} di_d + E_d \tag{15.9}$$

In the steady state the waveforms repeat with the time period T, and hence, $I_d(0) = I_d(T)$. Therefore, the average voltage across L_d in the steady state in Eq. (15.9) is zero.

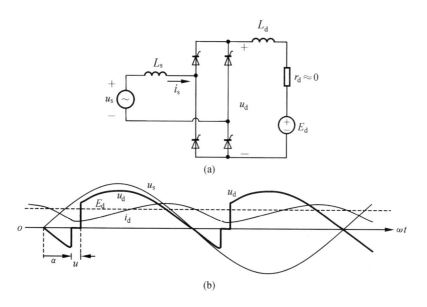

Fig. 15.5 A practical thyristor converter
(a) Circuit (b) Waveforms

In terms of average values, Eq. (15.9) can be written as

$$U_d = r_d I_d + E_d \tag{15.10}$$

In accordance with Eq. (15.7) we can control the average DC voltage U_d by means of α and thus control I_d and the power delivered to the load. The AC-side current waveforms associated with practical converters are analyzed by means of a computer simulation.

15.4 Inverter Mode of Operation

It was mentioned that the thyristor converters can also operate in an inverter mode, where U_d has a negative value, as shown in Fig. 15.1 (b), and hence the power flows from the DC side to the AC side. The easiest way to understand the inverter mode of operation is to assume that the DC side of the converter can be replaced by a current source of a constant amplitude I_d, as shown in Fig. 15.6(a). For a delay angle α greater than 90° but less than 180°, the voltage and current waveforms are shown in Fig. 15.6(b). The average value of u_d is negative, given by the equation $U_d = 0.9 U_s \cos\alpha - \dfrac{2}{\pi}\omega L_s I_d$, where $90° < \alpha < 180°$. Therefore, the average power $P_d (= U_d I_d)$ is negative, that is, it flows from the DC to the AC side. On the AC side, $P_{AC} = U_s I_{s1} \cos\varphi_1$ is also negative because $\varphi_1 > 90°$.

There are several points worth noting here. This inverter mode of operation is possible since there is a source of energy on the DC side. On the AC side, the AC voltage source facilitates the commutation of current from one pair of thyristors to another. The power flows into this AC source.

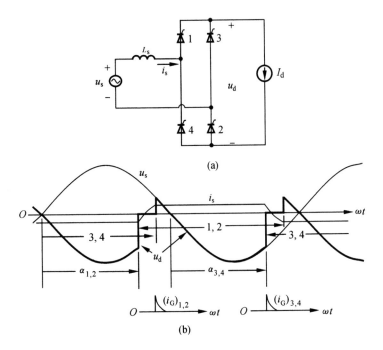

Fig. 15.6 Inverter assuming a constant DC current
(a) Circuit (b) Waveforms

Generally, the DC current source is not a realistic DC-side representation of systems where such a mode of operation may be encountered. Figure 15.7(a) shows a voltage source E_d on the DC side that may represent a battery, a photovoltaic source, or a DC voltage produced by a wind-electric system. It may also be encountered in a four-quadrant DC motor supplied by a back-to-back connected thyristor converter.

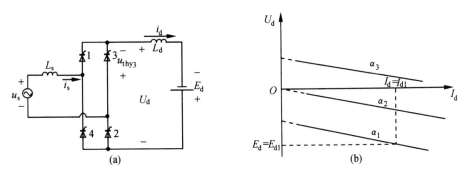

Fig. 15.7 Thyristor inverter with a DC voltage source
(a) Circuit (b) U_d versus I_d

An assumption of a very large value of L_d allows us to assume i_d to be a constant DC, and hence the waveforms of Fig. 15.6(b) also apply to the circuit of Fig. 15.7(a). Since the average voltage across L_d is zero,

$$E_d = U_d = U_{d0}\cos\alpha - \frac{2}{\pi}\omega L_s I_d \qquad (15.11)$$

The equation is exact if the current is constant at I_d; otherwise, a value of i_d at $\omega t = \alpha$ should be used in Eq. (15.11) instead of I_d. Figure 15.7(b) shows that for a given value of α, for example, α_1, the intersection of the DC source voltage $E_d = E_{d1}$, and the converter characteristic at α_1 determines the DC current I_{d1} and hence the power flow P_{d1}.

During the inverter mode, the voltage waveform across one of the thyristors is shown in Fig. 15.8. An extinction angle γ' is defined to be

$$\gamma' = 180° - (\alpha + \gamma) \tag{15.12}$$

during which the voltage across the thyristor is negative and beyond which it becomes positive[4]. As discussed in the above part dealing with thyristors, the extinction time interval $t_{\gamma} = \gamma'/\omega$ should be greater than the thyristor turn-off time t_q. Otherwise, the thyristor will prematurely begin to conduct, resulting in the failure of current to commutate from one thyristor pair to the other, an abnormal operation that can result in large destructive currents.

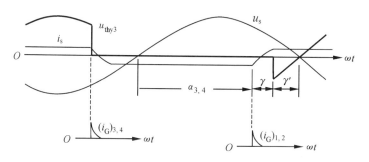

Fig. 15.8 Voltage across a thyristor in the inverter mode

🔍 New Words and Expressions

1. conversion *n.* 变换,转换
2. by means of 用,借助于
3. line-frequency *n.* 工频,电网频率
4. regenerative *adj.* 再生的
5. commutation *n.* 交换,换流
6. subset *n.* 子集
7. quadrant *n.* 象限
8. ripple *n.* 波纹
9. prior to 在……之前,先于
10. subsequent *adj.* 随后的,后来的
11. recognize *v.* 认可,接受
12. in accordance with 依照,根据
13. AC-side *n.* 交流侧
14. photovoltaic *adj.* 光电的,光伏的
15. intersection *n.* 交叉,交叉点
16. extinction *n.* 消灭,消失
17. prematurely *adv.* 过早地,贸然地
18. abnormal *adj.* 反常的,异常的
19. destructive *adj.* 破坏性的

Notes

1. Because of the large ripple in u_d and i_d, this circuit is of little practical significance.

   由于 u_d 和 i_d 有很大的脉动,所以这种电路几乎没有实际意义。

2. There is a finite commutation interval γ due to L_s.

   由于有 L_s(变压器漏感),因此存在一定的换相间隔 γ。

3. Also due to L_s and the ripple in i_d, the u_d waveform differs from the instantaneous $|u_s(t)|$ waveform by the voltage drop across L_s.

   也是因为考虑到 L_s 的存在及 i_d(流经负载的电流)波形中存在脉动,所以 u_d(负载两端的电压)波形为瞬时波形 $|u_s(t)|$ 减去 L_s 两端的压降。

4. An extinction angle γ' is defined to be
$$\gamma' = 180° - (\alpha + \gamma)$$
during which the voltage across the thyristor is negative and beyond which it becomes positive.

   extinction angle　消弧角

   消弧角定义为 $\gamma'=180°-(\alpha+\gamma)$,在消弧角区间内晶闸管两端承受的电压为负,超过消弧角区间则晶闸管两端承受的电压变为正。

Exercises

I. Translate the phrases into English.

1. 相控的　　2. 充电器　　3. 工频　　4. 变流器　　5. 整流
6. 逆变　　7. 可逆调速　　8. 再生制动　　9. 关断时间　　10. 纯电阻负载
11. 脉动　　12. 感性负载　　13. 周期　　14. 带内部直流电势的负载
15. 波形　　16. 换相　　17. 稳态　　18. 交流侧　　19. 延时角
20. 交点

II. Answer the following questions according to the text.

1. What is the relationship between the uncontrollable, line-frequency diode rectifiers and the controlled converters?
2. How does the power flow in the rectifier mode?
3. How is the inverter mode of operation possible?
4. How to implement the DC motor operation in all four quadrants?
5. What is the average voltage across L_d in the steady state equal to?
6. What is the range of a delay angle when the converter operates in the inverter mode?
7. What will happen when the extinction time interval is less than the thyristor turn-off time?

III. Translate the sentences into Chinese.

1. In these converters, the instant at which a thyristor begins or ceases to conduct depends on the line-frequency AC voltage waveforms and the control inputs.

2. In an inverter mode, U_d becomes negative (but I_d stays positive) and the power is transferred from the DC to the AC side.

3. Both the load voltage u_d and the current i_d have an average (DC) component.

4. Subsequent to $t=0$, the diode becomes forward biased and a current begins to flow.

5. After t_2, the input voltage u_s becomes negative but the current is still positive and the diode must conduct because of the inductor stored energy.

6. The current reaches its peak at t_2 (when u_s is again equal to E_d) and decays to zero at t_3, with t_3 determined by the requirement that the volt-second area A be equal to area B in the plot of u_L shown in Fig. 15.4(c).

7. This inverter mode of operation is possible since there is a source of energy on the DC side.

8. It may also be encountered in a four-quadrant DC motor supplied by a back-to-back connected thyristor converter.

Part 16

Basic Knowledge of Power System

16.1 Introduction

In this part we give a simplified description of a power system. The system consists of power sources, called *generating plants* (or *generators*), power end users, called *loads*, and a transmission and distribution network that connects them. Most commonly the generating plants convert energy from fossil or nuclear fuels, or from falling water, into electric energy.

16.2 Electric Energy

Electricity is only one of many forms of energy used in industry, homes, businesses, and transportation. It has many desirable features; it is clean (particularly at the point of use), convenient, relatively easy to transfer from point of source to point of use, and highly flexible in its use. In some cases it is an irreplaceable source of energy.

16.3 Fossil-Fuel Plant

In a fossil-fuel plant, coal, oil, or natural gas is burned in a furnace. The combustion produces hot water, which is converted to steam, and the steam drives a turbine, which is mechanically coupled to an electric generator. A schematic diagram of a typical coal-fired plant is shown in Fig. 16.1. In brief, the operation of the plant is as follows: Coal is taken from storage and fed to a pulverizer (or mill), mixed with preheated air, and blown into the furnace, where it is burned.

The furnace contains a complex of tubes and drums, called a *boiler*, through which water is pumped; the temperature of the water rises in the process until the water evaporates into steam. The steam passes on to the turbine, while the combustion gases (flue gases) are passed through mechanical and electrostatic precipitations, while removing upward of 99% of the solid particles (ash) before being releases to the chimney or stack.

The unit just described, with pulverized coal, air, and water as an input and steam as a useful output, is variously called a steam-generating unit, or furnace, or boiler. When the combustion process is under consideration, the term *furnace* is usually used, while the term *boiler* is more frequently used when the water-steam cycle is under consideration. The steam, at a typical pressure of 3500 psi and a temperature of 1050°F[1], is supplied through control and stop (shutoff) valves to the steam turbine. The control valve permits the output of the turbine-generator unit (or turbogenerator) to be varied by adjusting steam flow. The stop valve has a protective function; it is normally fully open but can be "tripped" shut to prevent overspeed of the turbine-generator unit if the electrical output drops suddenly (due to circuit breaker action) and the control valve does not close.

Figure 16.1 suggests a single-stage turbine, but in practice a more complex multi-stage arrangement is used to achieve relatively high thermal efficiencies.

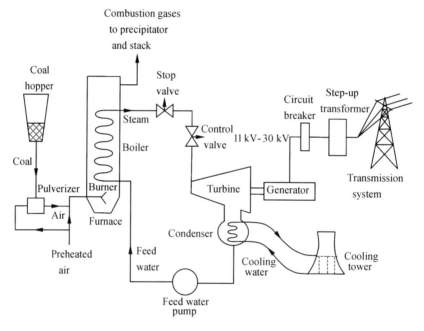

Fig. 16.1 Coal-fired power station (schematic)

16.4 Nuclear Power Plant

Controlled nuclear fission is the source of energy in a nuclear power plant. In the process of fission, heat is generated that is transferred to a coolant flowing through the reactor. Water is the most common coolant, but gases, organic compounds, liquid metals, and molten salts have also been used.

Although it might appear that the only difference between a nuclear plant and a fossil-fuel plant is the way the steam is produced (i.e., by nuclear reactor/steam generator rather than furnace/boiler), there are some other differences. For example, nuclear steam generators are presently limited in their temperature output to about 600°F (compared with about 1000°F for a fossil-fuel plant). This has a negative impact on thermal efficiency (30% instead of 40%) and on steam conditions in the turbines. There are, of course, major differences in the fuel cycle (supply and disposal) and in requirements for plant safety.

16.5 Hydroelectric Power Plant

Hydroelectric generation is an important source of power in the United States, accounting for approximately 14% of the installed generating capability and 11% of the energy production in 1996.

A highly desirable feature of hydropower plants can be noted: the speed with which they may be started up, brought up to speed, connected to the power network, and loaded up. This process can be done in under five minutes, in contrast to many hours in the case of thermal plants; the job is also much simpler and adaptable to remote control. Thus, hydropower is well suited for turning on and off at a dispatcher's command to meet changing power needs. When water is in short supply, it is desirable to use the limited available potential energy sparingly, for periods of short duration, to meet the peak-load demands. When water is plentiful, with the excess flowing over the spillway of the dam, base-loading use is indicated.

16.6 Other Energy Sources

There are additional energy sources currently used or under development. These include the following: gas turbines, biomass, geothermal energy, photovoltaic power, solar thermal energy, wind power, wastes as fuel, tidal power, ocean thermal energy conversion (OTEC), magnetohydrodynamic generation, generators driven by diesel engines, fuel cells, wave power, nuclear fusion, and the breeder reactor[2].

It is in the nature of some of these new sources (for example, photovoltaic and wind power) that they are of small size and widely dispersed geographically. To obtain the benefits of backup power and full utilization of the locally generated power and to eliminate the need for expensive local storage schemes, these small sources are best integrated into the utility network if feasible.

16.7 Transmission and Distribution Systems

The sources of electric power described in the preceding sections are usually interconnected by a transmission system or network that distributes the power to the various load points or load centers. A small portion of a transmission system that suggests the interconnections is shown as a one-line diagram in Fig. 16. 2. Various symbols for generators, transformers, circuit breakers, loads, and the points of connection (nodes), called *buses*, are identified in the figure.

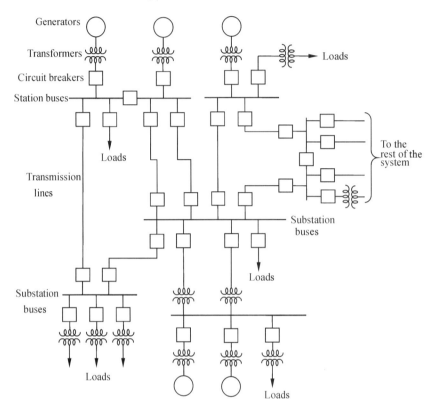

Fig. 16. 2　One-line diagram

The generator voltages are in the range of 11 to 30kV; higher generator voltages are difficult to obtain because of insulation problems in the narrow confines of the generator stator. Transformers are then used to step up the voltages to the range of 110 to 765kV. One reason for using high transmission-line voltage is to improve energy transmission efficiency. Another reason for higher voltages is the enhancement of stability.

A comment is in order about the loads shown in Fig. 16. 2. The loads referred to here represent bulk loads, such as the distribution system of a town, city, or large industrial plant. Such distribution systems provide power at various voltage levels. Large industrial consumers or railroads might accept power directly at voltage levels of 23 to 138kV; they would then step down the voltages further. Smaller industrials or commercial consumers typically accept power at voltage levels of 4. 16 to 34. 5kV. Residential consumers normally receive single-phase power from pole-mounted distribution transformers at voltage levels of 120/240V.

Although the transmission-distribution system is actually one interconnected system, it is convenient to separate the distribution system from the transmission system, as we have done in Fig. 16. 2. A similar diagram for the distribution system can be drawn with bulk substations replacing the generators as the sources of power and with lower-level loads replacing the bulk power loads shown in Fig. 16. 2.

16.8 Faults

Faults may have very serious consequences. At the fault point itself, there may be arcing, accompanied by high temperatures and, possibly, fire and explosion. There may be destructive mechanical forces due to very high currents. Overvoltages may stress insulation beyond the breakdown value[3]. Even in the case of less severe faults, high currents in the faulted system may overheat equipment; sustained overheating may reduce the useful life of the equipment. Clearly, faults must be removed from the system as rapidly as possible. In carrying out this objective an important, but secondary, objective is to remove no more of the system than absolutely necessary, in order to continue to supply as much of the load as possible. In this connection, we note that temporary loss of lighting or water pumping or air-conditioning load is not usually serious, but loss of service to some industrial loads can have serious consequences. Consider, for example, the problem of repair of an electric arc furnace in which the molten iron has solidified because of loss of power.

Faults are removed from a system by opening or "tripping" circuit breakers. These are the same circuit breakers used in normal system operation for connecting or disconnecting generators, lines, and loads. For emergency operation the breakers are tripped automatically when a fault condition is detected. Ideally, the operation is highly selective; only those breakers closest to the fault operate to remove or "clear" the fault. The rest of the system remains intact.

16.9 System Protection Components

Protection systems have three basic components:

① Instrument transformers; ② Relays; ③ Circuits breakers.

Figure 16. 3 shows a simple overcurrent protection schematic with: ① one type of instrument transformer—the current transformer (CT), ②an overcurrent relay (OC), and ③a circuit breaker (CB) for a single-phase line. The function of the CT is to reproduce in its secondary winding a current I' that is proportional to the primary current I. The CT converts primary currents in the kiloampere range to secondary currents in the 0-5 ampere range for convenience of measurement, with the following advantages.

Safety: Instrument transformers provide electrical isolation from the power system so that personnel working with relays will work in a safer environment.

Economy: Lower-level relay inputs enable relays to be smaller, simpler, and less expensive.

Accuracy: Instrument transformers accurately reproduce power system currents and voltages over wide operating ranges.

The function of the relay is to discriminate between normal operation and fault conditions. The OC relay in Fig. 16.3 has an operating coil, which is connected to the CT secondary winding, and a set of contacts. When $|I'|$ exceeds a specified "pickup" value, the operating coil causes the normally open contacts to close. When the relay contacts close, the trip coil of the circuit breaker is energized, which then causes the circuit breaker to open.

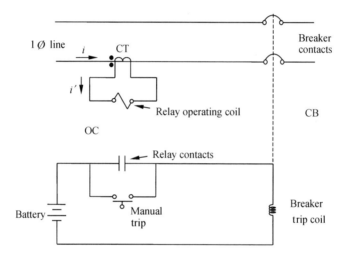

Fig. 16.3 Overcurrent protection schematic

Note that the circuit breaker does not open until its operating coil is energized, either manually or by relay operation. Based on information from instrument transformers, a decision is made and "relayed" to the trip coil of the breaker, which actually opens the power circuit—hence the name *relay*[4].

System-protection components have the following design criteria.

Reliability: Operate dependably when fault conditions occur, even after remaining idle for months or years. Failure to do so may result in costly damages.

Selectivity: Avoid unnecessary, false trips.

Speed: Operate rapidly to minimize fault duration and equipment damage. Any intentional time delays should be precise.

Economy: Provide maximum protection at minimum cost.

Simplicity: Minimize protection equipment and circuitry.

Since it is impossible to satisfy all these criteria simultaneously, compromises must be made in system protection.

New Words and Expressions

1. generating plant 发电厂，发电站
2. transmission network 输电网
3. distribution network 配电网
4. fossil fuel 化石燃料，矿物燃料
5. flexible *adj.* 灵活的，柔韧的
6. irreplaceable *adj.* 不能替代的
7. combustion *n.* 燃烧
8. turbine *n.* 涡轮
9. be coupled to 与……联结
10. schematic diagram 原理图
11. coal hopper 煤漏斗，煤斗
12. precipitator *n.* 除尘器
13. pulverizer *n.* 粉碎机
14. mill *n.* 磨粉机
15. drum *n.* 鼓
16. pump *v.* 抽吸
17. evaporate *v.* 蒸发，消失
18. flue gas 废气
19. electrostatic *adj.* 静电的
20. precipitation *n.* 沉淀，析出
21. ash *n.* 灰，灰烬
22. chimney (stack) *n.* 烟囱
23. pulverized coal 粉煤，煤粉
24. turbogenerator *n.* 涡轮式发电机
25. trip *v.* 自动断开
26. circuit breaker 断路器
27. nuclear fission 核裂变
28. coolant *n.* 冷冻剂，冷却剂
29. molten salt 熔盐
30. hydroelectric *adj.* 水力发电的
31. dispatcher *n.* 调度员，分配器
32. sparingly *adv.* 节俭地
33. spillway *n.* 溢水道，溢洪道
34. dam *n.* 水坝，水库
35. confine *n.* 范围，边界
36. substation *n.* 变电站，变电所
37. residential *adj.* 住宅的
38. fault *n.* 故障
39. arc *v.* 形成电弧 *n.* 电弧，弧形
40. destructive *adj.* 破坏的
41. current transformer 电流互感器
42. operating coil 合闸线圈
43. trip coil 跳闸线圈

Notes

1. psi＝pounds per square inch 磅/平方英寸（1psi＝0.068 标准大气压＝0.07 公斤力/平方厘米）

F 此处指华氏温标（Fahrenheit）。

2. There are additional energy sources currently used or under development. These include the following: gas turbines, biomass, geothermal energy, photovoltaic power, solar thermal energy, wind power, wastes as fuel, tidal power, ocean thermal energy conversion (OTEC), magnetohydrodynamic generation, generators driven by diesel engines, fuel cells, wave power, nuclear fusion, and the breeder reactor.

biomass *n.* 用作燃料或能源的生物质能

geothermal *adj.* 地热的

solar thermal 太阳能的

tidal *adj.* 潮汐的

magnetohydrodynamic *adj.* 磁流体动力(学)的

diesel engine 柴油机

fuel cell 燃料电池

nuclear fusion *n.* 核聚变

breeder reactor *n.* 增殖反应堆

现在有许多新的能源正在使用或开发中。这些新能源包括燃气发电、生物发电、地热发电、光伏发电、太阳能发电、风力发电、废弃燃料发电、潮汐发电、海洋热能发电、磁流体发电、柴油机发电、燃料电池发电、波浪发电、核聚变发电和增殖反应堆发电。

3. Overvoltages may stress insulation beyond the breakdown value.

过电压可能使绝缘体承受高于击穿值的电压。

4. Based on information from instrument transformers, a decision is made and "relayed" to the trip coil of the breaker, which actually opens the power circuit—hence the name *relay*.

根据互感器的信息进行决策,并将其传递给断路器的跳闸线圈,跳闸线圈切断电力电路——继电器由此得名。

Exercises

I. Translate the phrases into English.

1. 电力系统　　2. 发电厂　　3. 发电机　　4. 负荷　　5. 输电网
6. 配电网　　7. 电　　8. 天然气　　9. 原理图　　10. 锅炉
11. 热效率　　12. 风力　　13. 断路器　　14. 变电所　　15. 故障
16. 过电压　　17. 击穿值　　18. 过电流　　19. 可靠性　　20. 继电器
21. 触点　　22. 电流互感器　23. 合闸线圈　　24. 跳闸线圈

II. Answer the following questions according to the text.

1. What does the power system consist of?
2. What features does electricity have?
3. What interconnects the sources of electric power to the various load centers?
4. How many components do protection systems have? What are they?
5. What is the function of the CT?
6. What does the overcurrent protection use?

III. Translate the sentences into Chinese.

1. Faults are removed from a system by opening or "tripping" circuit breakers.

2. The function of the relay is to discriminate between normal operation and fault conditions.

3. The circuit breaker does not open until its operating coil is energized, either manually or by relay operation.

4. When the relay contacts close, the trip coil of the circuit breaker is energized, which then causes the circuit breaker to open.

科技英语学习要点(二)——科技英语翻译常用技巧

本部分将介绍科技英语翻译常用的五种技巧:转译法、省译法、增译法、还原法及倒置法。

2.1 Indirect Translation（转译法）

转译法主要有词类转译、句子成分转译两种。

- 词类转译

英语中,一个词类能充当的句子成分较少,充当不同成分时常需改变词类;而在汉语中,一个词类能充当的句子成分较多,充当不同句子成分时无须改变词类。因此,英汉翻译时,英语中的某种词类不一定译成汉语中的同一词类,往往根据汉语的习惯和需要转译成另一种词类,这就是词类的转译。

例如:

The *transformation* could be from any convenient input voltage to any convenient output voltage.

可将任一所需转换的输入电压转换成任一所希望的输出电压。（名词转译为汉语的动词）

Computers are more *flexible*, and can do a greater variety of jobs.

计算机的灵活性较大,因此,能做更多不同的工作。（形容词转译为汉语的名词）

An electric current *varies* directly as the electromotive force and inversely as the resistance.

电流的变化与电动势成正比,与电阻成反比。（动词转译为汉语的名词）

There are many substances *through* which electric currents will not pass at all.

有许多物质,电流是根本不能通过的。（介词转译为汉语的动词）

- 句子成分转译

句子成分转译的情况多种多样,方式可谓异彩纷呈。

例如:

These *electric machines* are well-designed structure.

这些电机的结构设计得很好。（主语转译为汉语的定语）

Fuzzy control *acts* differently from conventional PID control.

模糊控制的作用不同于传统的比例-积分-微分控制。（谓语转译为汉语的主语）

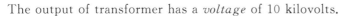

The output of transformer has a *voltage* of 10 kilovolts.
变压器的输出电压为10kV。（宾语转译为汉语的主语）
Rubber is a better *dielectric* but a poorer *insulator* than air.
橡胶的介电性比空气好,但绝缘性比空气差。（表语转译为汉语的主语）
There are three states *of matter* — solid, liquid and gas.
物质有三态:固态、液态和气态。（定语转译为汉语的主语）
It is stated *in Ohm's law* that the current flowing in a circuit is equal to the applied voltage divided by the resistance.
欧姆定律指出,电路中的电流等于外施电压除以电阻。（状语转译为汉语的主语）
Any body which is capable of doing work is considered to *possess* energy.
任何能做功的物体都具有能量。（补足语转译为汉语的谓语）
由于英汉两种语言的表达方式不同,因此,翻译时词语的意思有时也应做适当的转换。
例如:
Force and distance *measures* the amount of work.
力乘距离表示做功的大小。measure有"测定""估量"的意思,可转译为"表示"。

2.2 Omission Translation
（省译法）

英汉两种语言在遣词造句方面存在很大差异。英语中存在的词不一定能在汉语中找到与之相对应的词。英语句子中需要的词,汉语句子中不一定要出现。为使译文符合汉语的规范和习惯,翻译成汉语时应将一些不应出现在汉语中的词省略不译,这就是省译法。

省译法的原则是省词不省意,省译后应在内容上与原文保持一致。

• 冠词的省译

英语中的冠词是古英语中的指示代词和前置于名词的形容词的衍生词,属于虚词。它的基本功能是语法的,不是词义的。也就是说,冠词本身并没有独立的词汇意义。在现代英语中,它只是起一种指示范围的作用。因此,英语中的冠词在多数情况下是可以、也是应该省译的。

例如:
A transistor is *a* device controlling the flow of electricity in *a* circuit.
晶体管是电路中控制电流的器件。（不定冠词的省译）
The electric machine was invented in 1830's.
电机发明于19世纪30年代。（定冠词的省译）

• 代词的省译

英语中的代词包括人称代词、自身代词、物主代词、指示代词和关系代词等,翻译成汉语时可省略不译。

例如:
Insulators can also conduct electricity to some extent, though *they* give a high

resistance to an electric current.

虽然绝缘体对电流而言是很大的电阻,但多少也有一点导电性。(人称代词的省译)

Friction always manifests *itself* as a force that opposes motion.

摩擦总是表现为一种阻碍运动的力。(自身代词的省译)

Different metals differ in *their* conductivity.

不同的金属具有不同的导电性能。(物主代词的省译)

Series circuits do have the advantage of increasing resistance to reduce current when *this* is desirable.

串联电路的确有这样的优点:在需要时可以增加电阻来减少电流。(指示代词的省译)

The rate at *which* the electricity flows is measured in amperes.

电流的大小用安培度量。(关系代词的省译)

- 介词的省译

某些表示时间或地点的介词有时可省译。

例如:

In the transmission of electric power a high voltage is necessary.

输电必须用高压。

有时介词短语中的某些介词可省译。

例如:

The notebook computer carried *with* it the storage battery of itself.

笔记本自带蓄电池。

- 连词的省译

在许多情况下,英语连词的使用是一个语法规范问题,而汉语连词的使用则不涉及语法规范,多数是语气或习惯的问题,因此,翻译有连词的英语句式时,不能死抠原文,而应根据不同情况适当加以处理。在许多情况下连词可省译。

例如:

For every action there is an equal *and* opposite reaction.

对于每一个作用,都有一个大小相等、方向相反的反作用。(并列连词的省译)

Unless there is voltage, there is no current.

没有电压,就没有电流。(从属连词的省译)

- 动词的省译

英语的各类句型有一个共同的特点,就是必须有谓语动词(省略句另当别论)。汉语则不然,除了动词,形容词和名词等也可作谓语,因此翻译时动词有时可省译。

例如:

There *is* always some loss when a motor *is* working.

电动机运行时总有一定损耗。(系动词的省译)

Copper wire allows a larger current to flow than *does* iron wire.

铜导线比铁导线通过的电流大。(行为动词的省译)

- 名词的省译

英语中有时会出现充当主语的名词与充当表语或其他句子成分的名词相同的情况，翻译时出于修辞上的考虑，往往省略重复的名词。

例如：

Forces are measured in pounds, ounces, tons, grams, kilograms, and other *units* commonly called units of weight.

力由磅、盎司、吨、克、千克和其他一些常用重量单位度量。

- 同义词或近义词的省译

英语中有一物多名现象，因此，英语句中的某些词常常与其同义词或近义词连用，以表示同一事物的不同名称。汉语中虽然也有同义词或近义词现象，但那是指汉语中的某事物有多个汉语名称，而对于英语中的某事物也许就只有一个对应的叫法。因此，遇到英语中的同义词或近义词连用时，应视具体情况采用省译法。

例如：

As we know, electrons revolve about the *nucleus*, *or center*, of an atom.

众所周知，电子围绕着原子核旋转。

- 复数名词的省译

英语中的可数名词有单数和复数两种形式，可有些复数形式的名词就整个词而言并不是复数的概念。即便有些名词在英语中是复数概念，但翻译时也不一定要译出来，这就是复数名词的省译。

例如：

Mineral *oils* are very useful in industry.

矿物油在工业上很有用。

- 合并句子引起的省译

翻译时，有时会将两个单句合译成一个句子，或者将一个复合句译成一个单句，这时常常要省译其中的某些成分。

例如：

The electric current flows through a conductor as if *it were* a fluid.

电流像流体般流过导体。

2.3　Additional Translation
　　（增译法）

所谓增译法，就是英汉翻译时，在译文中增补一些在修辞、语法结构、语义或语气上必不可少的词。

- 复数名词译成汉语引起的增译

英语名词的复数一般通过其复数形式表示（一般在名词后加字母"s"），汉语则通过加数词或某些其他词的方式表示，因此，译成汉语时应增译某些表示复数的词，如"许多""若干""一些""一批""有些""各""诸"等。特别是当这些复数名词具有不可忽视的词义，若不译出就会造成误解或语义不全时,更应如此。

例如:

You must know the *properties* of the instrument before you use it.

在使用这种仪器前,必须弄清它的各种性能。

- 抽象名词译成汉语引起的增译

英语中有许多抽象名词,这些词若直译,不能表达具体明确的含义,因此,译成汉语时要加上"情况""作用""现象""效应""方法""过程""装置""设计"或"变化"等词。

例如:

Solution to the heating problem of the electric machine was ultimately found.

电机发热问题的解决方法终于找到了。

Integration can get rid of the static *error* in closed-loop system.

积分作用可消除闭环系统中的静差现象。

- 因添加量词引起的增译

英语是一种缺乏量词的语言,而汉语拥有丰富的量词,因此,翻译数词时往往要添加适当的量词,这样才能使译文符合汉语的规范。

例如:

There is an oil electric pump in the workshop.

车间里有一台电动油泵。

- 翻译省略成分引起的增译

英语最忌讳重复,凡前面出现的部分一般后面不再出现,以避免重复。但译成汉语时往往需将省略的部分增补上,这样才能使汉语语句完整。

例如:

Like charges repel each other, but opposite charges attract (each other).

同性电荷相互排斥,异性电荷相互吸引。

另外,英语语法规定,在某些句式中,有些成分往往要省略,但译成汉语时往往又需要将省略的部分增补上,否则意思就不完整。

例如:

This conclusion proved (to be) correct.

这一结论证明是正确的。

- 添加关联词引起的增译

在英语中,不少句式中的因果、转折及顺理连接等关系并不都是通过逻辑性语法词来表示的,而是通过语法习惯或用词习惯来体现的,因此,翻译此类句子时应增译某些关联词。

例如:

Being a good conductor, copper is generally used to conduct electricity.

由于铜是一种良导体,因此,一般用来导电。

- 添加表示时态的词引起的增译

英语有时态变化,而汉语没有,因此,译成汉语时要反映动作发生的时间,就需要增加某些表示时间的助词或副词。

例如：

This electric motor *is working* in full under the action of a heavy current.

在强电流的作用下，这台电机正满载运行。

- 添加概括性或分述性词语引起的增译

英语中在列举事实时很少用概括性的词语，在分述事物时也很少用分述性的词语，但汉语恰恰相反，因此，翻译时需根据情况增加一些概括性或分述性词语。

例如：

The chief effects of electric currents are the magnetic, heating, and chemical effects.

电流的主要效应有磁效应、热效应和化学效应三种。

- 翻译隐含意义引起的增译

英语中某些词的意思有时是隐含在其基本词义当中的，译成汉语时若不将这种意思讲明，便不能准确地表达句意。

例如：

This type of meter is called multimeter, which is used to measure *electricity*.

这种电表称为万用表，它是用来测量电量的。

- 翻译祈使句引起的增译

祈使句具有"命令""请求"或"叮咛"等含义，因此，翻译时应视不同情况添加"请""要""应""须""千万""一定"或"务必"等词语。

例如：

When the machine is in operation, do keep away from it.

机器运转时，请勿靠近。

Do be careful not to mix the liquids!

小心，切勿将这几种液体混在一起！

- 翻译某些动名词引起的增译

英语中的动名词虽是由动词变形而来的，但其动作性已高度抽象化了，翻译成具体动作时，应相应增译某些表达具体动作的动词。

例如：

Testing is a complicated problem, so be careful.

进行测试是一个复杂的问题，因此，得格外仔细。

- 翻译时为再现某些词引起的增译

例如：

Refrigerators, freezers and air-conditioning units must obey not only the First Law of Energy Conservation but the Second Law of Energy Conservation as well.

电冰箱、冷藏柜和空调装置不仅遵循能量守恒第一定律，而且遵循能量守恒第二定律。

Changing the number of turns of coils may step up or step down the voltage.

改变线圈匝数可升压，也可降压。

These are an ideal voltage source and current source.

这是一个理想电压源和一个理想电流源。

• 添加某些解释性词语引起的增译

英语中有些简称，译成汉语时应当解释清楚。

例如：

He bought a "586" yesterday.

昨天，他买了一台"586"计算机。

2.4 Reversion Translation
（还原法）

英语中为了避免重复，除了采取省略方法以外，还往往采用替代方法，使同一词语或句子成分不致重复出现。但在翻译时，因其替代关系并不一定能翻译清楚，或者汉语中根本就没有类似的表示方法，为了不致产生歧义，或者为了汉语行文上的需要，需译出所替代的原形，这就是还原法。

• 动词的还原

英语中为了避免重复使用同一动词，常用动词 do 替代前面出现过的动词。汉语中没有类似的用法，因此，需将动词还原。

例如：

In any case, work does not include time, but power *does*.

在任何情况下，功不包括时间，但功率却包括（时间）。

• 名词的还原

例如：

A diode can be used as a rectifier because in *it* the current flows in one direction.

二极管可用作整流器，因为电流在二极管中只朝一个方向流动。

While small generators frequently have revolving armatures, large *machines* usually have stationary armatures and revolving fields.

小型发电机常采用旋转电枢，而大型发电机常采用静止电枢和旋转磁场。

2.5 Inversion Translation
（倒置法）

英汉两种语言的语序有很大不同，英汉翻译时不能完全依照原文的语序，而应按照汉语的表达习惯，将原文的语序进行恰当的前后调整，以符合汉语行文的语法规范，这就是倒置法。

• 定语的倒置

英语的定语除由单个单词作定语时多数是前置的以外，其他的包括各种短语（不定式短语、介词短语、分词短语、形容词短语等）或从句作定语都是后置的。汉语正好相反，其定语基本都是前置的。因此，翻译时定语倒置是经常发生的。

例如:

An operational amplifier may be treated as a single electronic component *with input and output terminals*.

运算放大器可以看成是具有输入和输出端的单个电子元件。

Atomic energy is the greatest source of energy *existing*.

原子能是现存的最大能源。

英汉两种语言都存在两个或两个以上形容词修饰同一名词的语言现象,但其修饰语的语序是不同的。英语的语序是:先次要,再重要;先程度弱,再程度强;先小范围,再大范围;先一般,再专有。简单地说,就是越是重要的、越是代表其本质和身份的,就越靠近被修饰的名词,但汉语正好相反。因此,翻译时应将其语序倒置翻译。

例如:

They installed that *automatic thermal* regulator yesterday.

昨天他们安装了那台温度自动调节器。

- 状语的倒置

英语中,修饰动词的状语一般在所修饰的动词之后,即状语一般是后置的,而汉语正好相反,因此,此时应采用倒置译法。

例如:

Electric power can be transmitted over distant places *along cables*.

电能可通过电缆远距离送电。

类似于定语,状语也存在语序的问题。英语状语出现的次序是先方式状语,再地点状语,最后是时间状语,而汉语正好相反。

例如:

It is our task to build up a chemical plant station *somewhere* *by the end of this year*.
                                                    地点   时间

我们的任务是于今年年底在某地建成一座化工厂。
              时间   地点

- 同位语的倒置

英语中的同位语,特别是同位语从句,往往处于被修饰词之后,但译成汉语时常常前置。

例如:

The discovery *that electric current can be produced by magnetism* is extremely important in the field of electricity.

电流由磁产生,这一发现对电领域是极其重要的。

- 主语的倒置

疑问句、there be 句型和倒装句在翻译时主语都应倒置。

例如:

With the velocity of light *travel electromagnetic waves*.

电磁波以光速传播。

- 宾语的倒置

英译汉时,有时为了突出宾语所表示的事物,或是为使译文更符合汉语表达习惯,往往将宾语倒置翻译。

例如：

We are glad to accept *your new technique*.

你的新工艺,我们乐于采纳。

- 并列成分的倒置

当并列连词 as well as 连接并列的两个成分时,其所强调的是前者而不是后者,但汉语习惯于将所强调的内容后置,因此,翻译时应先译后者,再译前者。

例如：

We can turn electric energy into light energy as well as *into heat energy*.

我们不仅能将电能转换成热能,还能将其转换成光能。

- 修饰词与被修饰词的倒置

英语的名词性修饰词与被修饰的名词之间的前后关系有些与汉语的正好相反,因此,翻译时应倒置。

例如：

The *speed necessary* is 3000 r/min.

所需转速为 3000 r/min。

- 复合词的词序倒置

英语中复合词的组词词序有些与相应的汉语组词词序正好相反,因此,译成汉语时应倒置。

例如：

| northeast | 东北 | water-proof | 防水的 |
| light-tight | 不透光的 | | |

- 习语的词序倒置

有些英语的习语其词序与相应的汉语词序并不相同,因此,译成汉语时应倒置。

例如：

| sooner or later | 迟早 | right and left | 左右 |
| one and the same | 同一的 | one and only | 唯一的 |

练习参考答案

Part 1

I. Translate the phrases into English.

1. electric circuit
2. electrical engineering
3. electric machine
4. physical science
5. electrical device
6. electrical element
7. positive charge
8. negative charge
9. direct current
10. alternating current
11. voltage
12. conductor
13. work
14. electromotive force
15. potential difference
16. power
17. polarity
18. the law of conservation of energy

II. Answer the following questions according to the text.

1. It is the electric charge.
2. It is mobile.
3. The motion of charges creates an electric current.
4. A DC is a current that remains constant with time.
5. An AC is a current that varies sinusoidally.
6. Power is being delivered to the element.

III. Translate the sentences into Chinese.

1. 电路是电气元件的相互连接。
2. 电流是电荷对时间的变化率。
3. 电压（或电势差）是在元件中移动一个单位的电荷所需的能量，其量纲为伏。
4. 功率是消耗或吸收的能量对时间的变化率，其量纲为瓦。
5. 一个元件吸收或供给的功率等于元件两端的电压与流经元件的电流之积。
6. 能量为做功的能力，其量纲为焦耳。
7. 供给电路的总功率一定等于电路所吸收的总功率。

Part 2

I. Translate the phrases into English.

1. variable
2. resistance
3. resistivity
4. insulator
5. resistor
6. passive element

7. constant	8. conductance	9. short circuit
10. open circuit	11. linear	12. series
13. parallel	14. voltage drop	15. equivalent resistance

II. **Answer the following questions according to the text.**

1. It states that the voltage across a resistor is directly proportional to the current flowing through the resistor.

2. A short circuit is a circuit element with resistance approaching zero.

3. An open circuit is a circuit element with resistance approaching infinity.

4. It obeys Ohm's law.

5. Because it always absorbs power from the circuit.

6. Yes, because a node may be regarded as a closed surface shrunk to a point.

7. They are connected sequentially, end to end.

8. They are connected to the same two nodes.

III. **Translate the sentences into Chinese.**

1. 元件的电阻 R 表示其阻碍电流流动的能力,其量纲为欧姆(Ω)。

2. 基尔霍夫电流定律 KCL 表明,流进一个节点(或一条封闭路径)的电流的代数和为零。

3. 如果若干个电流源并联,则总的电流为各个电流源电流的代数和。

4. 基尔霍夫电压定律 KVL 表明,沿着一条封闭路径的总电压的代数和为零。

5. 若干个电压源串联时,应用基尔霍夫电压定律就可以得到总的电压。总的电压为各个电压源电压的代数和。

6. 若干个电阻串联之后的等效电阻为各个电阻之和。

Part 3

I. **Translate the phrases into English.**

1. capacitor	2. inductor	3. storage element
4. electric field	5. charge	6. discharge
7. dynamic	8. dielectric	9. capacitance
10. magnetic field	11. power supply	12. transformer
13. electric motor	14. coil	15. inductance
16. conducting wire	17. winding	18. leakage resistance

II. **Answer the following questions according to the text.**

1. Because they do not dissipate but store energy, which can be retrieved at a later time.

2. Current flows into the positive terminal of the capacitor.

3. Because the capacitor voltage depends on the past history of the capacitor current.

4. Because a DC voltage is not changing with time, the current through the capacitor

is zero.

5. Because a DC current is not changing with time, the voltage across an inductor is zero.

III. Translate the sentences into Chinese.

1. 电容定义为电容器一片金属板上的电荷与两板之间的电压差之比,其量纲为法拉。

2. 电容两端的电压不能突变。

3. 如果有电流流经电感,则电感两端的电压与该电流对时间的变化率成正比。

4. 令 $i(-\infty)=0$ 是实际的、合理的,因为在过去一定存在一个使流经电感的电流为零的时间。

5. 电感具有与通过它的电流变化相反的重要特性。

Part 4

I. Translate the phrases into English.

1. cost of computing	2. microprocessor	3. search engine
4. hardware	5. software	6. program
7. data storage	8. peripheral	9. communication
10. instruction	11. control unit	12. central processing unit
13. system bus	14. code	15. arithmetic and logic unit
16. read-write memory	17. configuration	18. addressable
19. register	20. supercomputer	21. server
22. database	23. consumer-oriented	24. decoder
25. embedded computer		

II. Answer the following questions according to the text.

1. A computer can perform data processing, data storage, data movement, and control.

2. A computer consists mainly of four main parts. They are CPU, main memory, I/O, and system connection.

3. The software is referred to as a sequence of codes or instructions.

4. I/O buffer (I/O BR) register is used for the exchange of data between an I/O module and the CPU.

5. The server can usually be accessed only via a network.

6. Because the results can vary from upsetting to devastating.

III. Translate the sentences into Chinese.

1. 即使计算机正在动态地处理数据,计算机也至少要临时存储特定时刻正在处理的那些数据。

2. 直接连接到计算机的设备接收或发送数据的过程就是输入-输出(I/O),该设备被称为外设。

3. 在计算机内部，控制单元管理计算机的资源，并根据那些指令协调其功能部件的性能。

4. 中央处理单元（CPU）控制计算机的操作并执行其数据处理功能；通常简称为处理器。

5. 内存模块由一组被顺序编号的地址所标识的位置组成。每个位置包含一条指令或数据对应的二进制数。

6. 个人电脑着重考虑的是以低成本向单个用户提供性能良好的机器，通常执行第三方软件。

7. 构建服务器的基本技术与台式计算机相同，但是服务器提供了更强大的计算、存储和输入/输出能力。

Part 5

I. Translate the phrases into English.

1. operational amplifier 2. active circuit 3. electronic unit
4. package 5. pin 6. noninverting terminal
7. inverting input 8. circuit diagram
9. voltage-controlled voltage source 10. open-loop gain
11. closed-loop gain 12. negative feedback 13. positive saturation
14. linear region 15. voltage follower 16. equivalent impedance

II. Answer the following questions according to the text.

1. An op amp can sum signals, amplify a signal, integrate it, or differentiate it. The ability of the op amp to perform these mathematical operations is the reason why it is so called.

2. Because they are versatile, inexpensive, easy to use, and fun to work with.

3. Yes. Because the op amp must be powered by a voltage supply.

4. When there is a feedback path from output to input, the closed-loop gain is the ratio of the output voltage to the input voltage.

5. There are three modes. They are positive saturation, linear region and negative saturation.

6. An ideal op amp is an amplifier with infinite open-loop gain, infinite input resistance, and zero output resistance.

7. The current into each of its two input terminals is zero, and the voltage across its input terminals is negligibly small.

8. It is a noninverting amplifier.

III. Translate the sentences into Chinese.

1. 运算放大器是能完成加、减、乘、除、微分和积分这些数学运算的有源电路元件。

2. 输出部分包括一个压控电压源和一个与之串联的电阻 R。

3. 运算放大器检测到两输入的差,放大 A 倍,在输出端产生相应的电压。

4. 两输入端间的电阻为无穷大就意味着两输入端为开路,没有电流流进运算放大器。

5. 在这个电路中,同相输入端接地,u_i 通过 R_1 与反相输入端相连,反馈电阻 R_f 连到输入和输出之间。

6. 在反相放大器中,输出电压为负的输入电压的倍数。

7. 电压跟随器将两级之间的影响减至最小并消除了级间的加载。

Part 6

I. Translate the phrases into English.

1. logic variable
2. bit
3. digital word
4. byte
5. nibble
6. AND operation
7. truth table
8. AND gate
9. NOT gate
10. OR gate
11. addition sign
12. NAND gate
13. XOR operation
14. logic expression
15. binary system
16. positive logic
17. negative logic
18. reference direction

II. Answer the following questions according to the text.

1. A byte is a word consisting of eight bits. A nibble is a four-bit word.

2. It is the circuit that performs the NOT operation.

3. It is called Boolean algebra.

4. The NAND gate.

5. Buffers are used to provide large currents when a logic signal must be applied to a low-impedance load.

III. Translate the sentences into Chinese.

1. 真值表就是关于逻辑运算的所有输入和输出的一张表。

2. 在逻辑变量符号上加一根短横表示逻辑非运算。

3. 缓冲器只有一个输入,并且产生与输入相同的输出。

4. 只有两个输入相同时,等效门才输出高。实际上,等效门为异或门后加上一个反相器。

5. 如果将逻辑表达式中的变量用其相反变量代替,与门换成或门,或门换成与门,表达式再取反,则所得的逻辑表达式的值与原表达式的值是相同的。

6. 若电流从输出端流出(I_O 为负),称反相器产生电流。另一方面,若电流流进输出端,则称输出端吸收电流。

Part 7

I. Translate the phrases into English.

1. ideal transformer
2. electrical isolation
3. impedance matching
4. electrical power
5. isolating transformer
6. voltage transformer

7. current transformer   8. primary winding   9. operating frequency
10. distribution transformer   11. power transformer   12. flux density
13. magnetic field   14. iron-core transformer   15. high-power
16. air-core   17. magnetic coupling   18. lower-power
19. magnetizing loss   20. hysteresis loss   21. eddy current
22. exciting current   23. leakage flux   24. mutual flux
25. coil   26. core-type   27. shell-core
28. high-voltage winding   29. flux linkage   30. electromotive force(emf)
31. root mean square (rms) value   32. turns ratio
33. apparent power   34. the number of turns   35. step-up transformer
36. step-down transformer

II. Answer the following questions according to the text.

1. Because it has no moving parts.

2. They are used to electrically isolate electric circuits from each other or to block DC signals while maintaining AC continuity between the circuits, and to eliminate electromagnetic noise in many types of circuits.

3. Distribution transformers. Power transformers.

4. It is the ratio of the number of turns of the primary winding to the number of turns of the secondary winding.

5. The potential ratio is equal to the turns ratio.

6. The primary and secondary turns of the isolating transformer are equal.

The number of turns of the secondary winding is greater than the number of turns of the primary winding of a step-up transformer.

The number of turns of the primary winding is greater than the number of turns of the secondary winding of a step-down transformer.

III. Translate the sentences into Chinese.

1. 变压器通常用于改变给定电气系统中电压和电流的等级、进行电气隔离、实现阻抗匹配和测量仪器。

2. 电压互感器是单相变压器,它用于将被测量电压降至安全值。电流互感器用于减小电流至可测量等级。

3. 小写字母用于表示瞬时值,大写字母用于表示有效值。

4. 设计良好的新式变压器其铁芯的磁阻在铁芯饱和前很小(几乎为零)。

5. 流经绕组中的电流与绕组的匝数成反比。

Part 8

I. Translate the phrases into English.

1. motor   2. generator   3. mechanical energy

4. electrical energy	5. electromagnetic	6. linear motor
7. synchronous machine	8. induction machine	9. stator
10. rotor	11. air gap	12. shaft
13. armature	14. field winding	15. reactive power
16. braking mode	17. steady-state	18. phase sequence
19. plugging	20. lagging current	21. magnetizing reactance
22. starting current	23. frequency changer	24. induced voltage
25. inverter	26. cycloconverter	27. commutator

II. Answer the following questions according to the text.

1. A motor is the machine which is used to convert electrical energy into mechanical energy.

A generator is the machine that is used to convert mechanical energy into electrical energy.

2. Because it has the advantages of relatively low cost, simple and rugged construction, minimal maintenance requirements, and good operating characteristics which satisfy a wide variety of loads.

3. The rotating field passing through the loops in the rotor always turns more slowly than the rotating field.

4. Because no current has to be supplied to the rotor.

5. An induction machine can be operated in three regions. They are the motor region, generator region, and braking region.

6. They are generated by three-phase synchronous machines operated as generators.

7. They can provide constant mechanical power output or constant torque, adjustable motor speed over wide ranges, precise speed or position control, efficient operation over a wide speed range, rapid acceleration and deceleration, and responsiveness to feedback signals.

8. It is a function of the flux in the machine, the speed of its rotor, and a constant that depends on the machine.

III. Translate the sentences into Chinese.

1. 电机是当发电机使用还是当电动机使用决定与机械系统相连的转动部分是接收机械输入还是提供机械输出。

2. 转子位于定子的中心,转子和定子之间的空间被称为气隙。

3. 感应电机运行在电动状态时,其转速略低于同步转速;而运行在发电状态时,其转速略高于同步转速,这就需要从与之相连的系统向电源提供励磁的无功功率。

4. 因为感应电机不能产生激励,所以它需要无功功率;它从电源吸入一个滞后的电流,在功率因数小于1(通常大于0.85)下运行。

5. 给三相定子绕组加三相电压就会产生旋转的磁场,该磁场以电源频率 f_1 "切割"定子和转子绕组。

6. 外部直流电源通过滑环和电刷向转子绕组供电,从而产生转子磁场。

7. "同步"指在稳态运行时电机以恒定的转速和频率运行。

8. 加号用于发电机,减号用于电动机。发电机的电枢电压总是高于端电压。电动机的电枢电压低于端电压。

Part 9

I. Translate the phrases into English.

1. independent variable   2. speech signal   3. density
4. continuous-time signal   5. discrete-time signal   6. integer
7. sequence   8. successive sample   9. velocity
10. grid   11. brightness   12. periodic signal
13. fundamental period   14. even signal   15. odd signal
16. unit impulse   17. unit step   18. function
19. first difference   20. derivative   21. integral
22. response   23. periodicity

II. Answer the following questions according to the text.

1. The independent variable takes on only a discrete set of values.

2. We usually use the symbol t to denote the continuous-time independent variable and n to denote the independent variable.

3. The property is unchanged by a time shift of T.

4. An even signal is identical to its time-reversed counterpart. An odd signal is opposite to its time-reversed counterpart.

5. Because any real physical system has some inertia associated with it.

III. Translate the sentences into Chinese.

1. 对于连续时间信号,自变量是连续的,因此这些信号被限定为自变量的连续值。

2. 具体来说,一个离散时间信号 $x[n]$ 如果时间移动 N 后仍不变,那么这个信号 $x[n]$ 就是周期为 N 的周期信号,其中 N 是正整数。

3. 重要的事实是任何信号都可以被分解成两个信号的和,一个是偶信号,一个是奇信号。

4. 特别地,离散时间单位脉冲是离散时间阶跃的一阶差分。反之,离散时间单位阶跃是单位脉冲(或取样)的求和。

5. 连续时间单位阶跃是单位脉冲的积分函数。连续时间单位脉冲可以看作连续时间单位阶跃的一阶导数。

6. 单位脉冲是"脉冲对于任何系统来说都足够短的"这个概念的理想化。

Part 10

I. Translate the phrases into English.

1. high-fidelity
2. series(cascade)
3. block diagram
4. parallel
5. feedback
6. accumulator
7. delay
8. clock pulse
9. causality
10. stability
11. diverge
12. time invariant
13. stable system
14. unstable
15. nonlinear
16. superposition
17. complex constant
18. additivity
19. scaling
20. homogeneity

II. Answer the following questions according to the text.

1. The output of the former system is the input to the later system in the series interconnection of two systems.

The same input signal is applied to the parallel interconnection of two systems.

2. A resistor is a memoryless system and a capacitor is an example of a continuous-time system with memory.

3. Because the output of these systems responds only to the current value of the input.

4. Responses will diverge.

5. They are the additivity property and the scaling or homogeneity property.

III. Translate the sentences into Chinese.

1. 广义上的实体系统是元件、装置或子系统的相互连接。

2. 系统可以被看作是一个过程，在这个过程中系统将输入信号进行转换，或者以某种方式对输入信号做出响应，从而产生输出信号。

3. 系统1的输出是系统2的输入，系统2的输出被反馈回输入端并与外部输入叠加后作为系统1的实际输入。

4. 如果系统在给定时间内对自变量的每个值的输出只与当前的输入有关，那么系统就是无记忆的。

5. 如果任何时刻的输出仅依赖于输入的当前值和过去值，那么系统就是因果的。

6. 较为正式的对稳定性的定义是，如果一个稳定系统的输入是有界的（如果其大小没有无限制地增长），则输出也一定是有界的，因此系统不可能发散。

7. 如果输入信号的时移使输出信号产生相同的时移，则该系统是时不变的。

8. 连续时间或离散时间的线性系统均具有重要的叠加性质。

Part 11

I. Translate the phrases into English.

1. automatic control
2. controller
3. disturbance
4. desired value
5. pressure
6. liquid level
7. controlled variable
8. block diagram
9. transfer function
10. process control
11. servomechanism
12. flow rate
13. acceleration
14. forward path
15. correction
16. feedback path
17. closed-loop
18. open-loop
19. output
20. gain
21. manual adjustment
22. transducer
23. error
24. control mode
25. proportional control
26. integral control
27. derivative control
28. manipulating element
29. settling time
30. residual error

II. Answer the following questions according to the text.

1. A control system is a group of components that maintains a desired result by manipulating the value of another variable in the system.

2. It is defined as the ratio of the Laplace transform of the output signal divided by the Laplace transform of the input signal.

3. It is also a sinusoidal signal.

4. It is the ratio of the amplitude of the output signal divided by the amplitude of the input signal.

5. It is less expensive than closed-loop control. The controller is much simpler.

6. It can compute the difference between the measured value of the controlled variable and the desired value (or set point).

7. There are three modes. They are the proportional mode (P), the integral mode (I), and the derivative mode (D).

8. It maintains the controlled variable exactly equal to the set point at all times, regardless of load changes or set point changes.

III. Translate the sentences into Chinese.

1. 元件的传递函数描述了输出信号与输入信号间的大小和时间关系。
2. 反馈的作用是测量实际值与期望值之差,并利用这个差向期望值方向调节实际值。
3. 测量传感器对被控量进行检测,并将其转换为有用信号。
4. 决策操作计算误差(期望值减去被测量值),并利用该误差形成控制动作。执行操作则使用此控制动作向减小误差的方向控制过程中的一些变量。
5. 减小残差的问题可以通过增大控制器的增益来解决,因此,需要一个较小的残差来产生必要的校正控制动作。

Part 12

I. Translate the phrases into English.

1. uncertainty
2. observation
3. sample
4. arithmetic average (mean)
5. expected value
6. standard deviation
7. lower range limit
8. upper range limit
9. span
10. resolution
11. dead band
12. sensitivity
13. threshold
14. reliability
15. overrange
16. recovery time
17. overload
18. overrange limit
19. drift
20. accuracy
21. error
22. repeatability
23. systemic error
24. reproducibility
25. calibration
26. linear velocity
27. angular velocity
28. radian
29. tachometer
30. incremental encoder
31. timed counter
32. stability

II. Answer the following questions according to the text.

1. It is to obtain the true value of the measured variable.

2. The span is the difference between the upper range limit and the lower range limit.

3. It is threshold.

4. Sensitivity refers to static values, whereas gain usually refers to the amplitude of sinusoidal signals.

5. Overrange is any excess in the value of the measured variable above the upper range limit or below the lower range limit.

6. It includes hysteresis, dead band, drift, and repeatability.

7. It is the rate of change of displacement or distance.

8. There are three. They are DC tachometers, AC tachometers, and optical tachometers..

III. Translate the sentences into Chinese.

1. 当对变量进行测量时，就存在不确定性。

2. 采样平均值是对下一个观测数据期望值的估计。对观测数据求和并除以观测数据个数就可以计算出平均值。

3. 决策操作计算误差（期望值减去被测值），并用此误差形成控制动作。

4. 量程包括下限和上限之间的所有值。

5. 准确性指测量仪器的输出值与某种标准确定的被测量理想值之间的一致程度。

6. 重复性是在全量程范围内，对同一个输入从同一个方向逼近时连续输出之间的最大差值。

7. 角速度为角位移对时间的变化率。

8. 交流测速仪是输出带有一个三相整流器的三相发电机。

Part 13

I. Translate the phrases into English.

1. interface
2. conditioner
3. switch
4. actuator
5. solenoid valve
6. sequential control system
7. contact
8. normally open
9. normally closed
10. limit switch
11. relay
12. time-delay relay
13. pull-in current
14. drop-out current
15. motor starter
16. contactor
17. holding contact
18. rectifier
19. converter
20. inverter
21. diode
22. anode
23. cathode
24. forward biased
25. reverse biased
26. block
27. zener diode
28. transistor
29. collector
30. base
31. emitter
32. common-emitter
33. triac
34. positive half-cycle
35. trigger circuit

II. Answer the following questions according to the text.

1. They are devices that make or break the connection in an electric circuit.

2. One or more pairs of contacts.

3. It is a set of switches that are actuated when electric current passes through a coil of wire.

4. Normally open contacts.

5. A motor starter; a contactor.

6. They are used as rectifiers in DC power supplies and as one-way "valves" to block or bypass undesired electric currents.

7. It is forward biased.

8. They are used as switches, amplifiers, and oscillators.

9. It is that the triac can conduct in both directions, whereas the SCR can conduct in only one direction.

III. Translate the sentences into Chinese.

1. 控制器与它所控制的过程有两个接口,一个是加到控制器的输入,另一个是来自于控制器的输出。

2. 常闭触点用由一根斜线连接的两根平行线表示。

3. 在延时继电器中,延时发生在箭头所指的方向。

4. 当继电器线圈通电时,常闭触点断开电路通道;若继电器线圈断电,常闭触点将接通电路通道。

5. 三个大功率触点用于开、关给负载供电的三相电网,二个小功率触点用在控制电路中。

6. 通过在可控硅整流器的门极施加短脉冲的控制电流,就可以使其导通,并且只要有电流从其阳极流向阴极,可控硅整流器就会一直导通。

Part 14

I. Translate the phrases into English.

1. power capability   2. power device   3. thyristor
4. conduction   5. forward-blocking   6. on-state
7. off-state   8. reverse breakdown voltage
9. leakage current   10. current rating   11. drain
12. gate   13. snubber circuit   14. current sharing
15. rated voltage   16. controllable switch

II. Answer the following questions according to the text.

1. They are the increased power capabilities, ease of control, and reduced costs.

2. When a pulse of positive gate current is applied for a short duration provided that the device is in its forward-blocking state.

3. Only when the anode current tries to go negative.

4. It is Metal-Oxide-Semiconductor Field Effect Transistor.

5. It can be turned off by applying a negative gate-cathode voltage.

6. In order to allow the current to flow in the reverse direction.

7. It is Insulated Gate Bipolar Transistor.

III. Translate the sentences into Chinese.

1. 晶闸管处于关断状态时能承受一个正向的电压但却不导通。

2. 当栅极和源极电压大于阈值电压时,器件饱和导通,近似为一个闭合的开关。

3. GTO 能承受负的电压,这个电压的大小取决于 GTO 的设计。

4. 因为 GTO 能承受高电压(高达 4.5kV)和大电流(高达几千安),所以当需要开、关频率在几百赫兹到 10 千赫兹范围内能承受高压、大电流的开关时,就可以采用 GTO。

Part 15

I. Translate the phrases into English.

1. phase-controlled   2. charger   3. line-frequency
4. converter   5. rectification   6. inversion
7. reversible-speed   8. regenerative braking   9. turn-off time
10. pure resistive load   11. ripple   12. inductance load
13. time period   14. load with an internal DC voltage
15. waveform   16. commutation   17. steady state
18. AC-side   19. delay angle   20. intersection

II. Answer the following questions according to the text.

1. The uncontrollable, line-frequency diode rectifiers are a subset of the controlled converters.

2. The power flow is from the AC to the DC side.

3. Only if a source of power, such as batteries, is present on the DC side.

4. This is accomplished by connecting two two-quadrant converters in antiparallel or back to back.

5. Zero.

6. It is greater than 90° but less than 180°.

7. The thyristor will prematurely begin to conduct, resulting in the failure of current to commutate from one thyristor pair to the other.

III. Translate the sentences into Chinese.

1. 在这些变换器中,晶闸管开始导通或关断的时刻取决于工频交流电压的波形和控制输入信号。

2. 在逆变方式下 U_d 为负(但 I_d 依然为正),功率从直流侧向交流侧传递。

3. 负载电压 u_d 和电流 i_d 都含有直流分量。

4. 在 $t=0$ 之后,二极管处于正向偏置,电流开始流经二极管。

5. t_2 时刻以后,输入电压 u_s 变为负,但电流还为正;由于电感中储存了能量,二极管还处于导通状态。

6. 在 t_2 时刻,电流达到峰值(当 u_s 又等于 E_d 时);在 t_3 时刻,电流衰减为零。由图15.4 (c)中 u_L 曲线可见,电压和时间所围的面积 A 等于 B 的时刻决定了 t_3 时刻。

7. 因为在直流侧有能源,所以这种逆变运行方式是可能的。

8. 可能会在由反并联连接的晶闸管变流器供电的直流电动机四象限运行中碰到。

Part 16

I. Translate the phrases into English.

1. power system	2. generating plant	3. generator
4. load	5. transmission network	6. distribution network
7. electricity	8. natural gas	9. schematic diagram
10. boiler	11. thermal efficiency	12. wind power
13. circuit breaker	14. substation	15. fault
16. overvoltage	17. breakdown value	18. overcurrent
19. reliability	20. relay	21. contact
22. current transformer	23. operating coil	24. trip coil

II. Answer the following questions according to the text.

1. It consists of power sources, loads, and a transmission and distribution network.

2. It has many features: It is clean, convenient, relatively easy to transfer from point

of source to point of use, and highly flexible in its use.

3. A transmission system or network usually distributes the power to points or load centers.

4. There are three. They are instrument transformers, relays, and circuit breakers.

5. The function of the CT is to reproduce in its secondary winding a current that is proportional to the primary current.

6. The overcurrent protection uses the current transformer, an overcurrent relay, and a circuit breaker.

III. Translate the sentences into Chinese.

1. 通过使断路器跳闸可将故障从系统中排除。
2. 继电器的作用是区分正常运行和故障情况。
3. 通过手动或使用继电器控制,使断路器的合闸线圈通电,这时断路器合闸。
4. 当继电器的触头闭合时,断路器的跳闸线圈通电,从而将断路器分闸。

References

[1] Alexander C K, Sadiku M N O. Fundamentals of Electric Circuits[M]. 2nd ed. Singapore: McGraw-Hill, Inc., 2004.

[2] Stallings W. Computer Organization and Architecture Designing for Performance[M]. 9th ed. New Jersey: Pearson Education, Inc., 2013.

[3] Hambley A R. Electronics[M]. 2nd ed. 北京:高等教育出版社,2004.

[4] Gönen T. Electrical Machines[M]. California: Power International Press, 1998.

[5] 戴文进. 科技英语翻译理论与技巧[M]. 上海:上海外语教育出版社,2003.

[6] Oppenheim A V, Willsky A S, Nawab S H. Signals & Systems[M]. 2nd ed. New Jersey: Prentice-Hall, Inc., 1996.

[7] Bateson R N. Introduction to Control System Technology[M]. 7th ed. 北京:机械工业出版社,2006.

[8] Mohan N, Undeland T M, Robbins W P. Power Electronics: Converters, Applications and Design[M]. 3rd ed. 北京:高等教育出版社,2004.

[9] Bergen A R, Viuttal V. Power Systems Analysis[M]. 2nd ed. 北京:机械工业出版社,2005.